LONGING FOR SPRING

NML NEW MONASTIC LIBRARY
Resources for Radical Discipleship

For over a millennium, if Christians wanted to read theology, practice Christian spirituality, or study the Bible, they went to the monastery to do so. There, people who inhabited the tradition and prayed the prayers of the church also copied manuscripts and offered fresh reflections about living the gospel in a new era. Two thousand years after the birth of the church, a new monastic movement is stirring in North America. In keeping with ancient tradition, new monastics study the classics of Christian reflection and are beginning to offer some reflections for a new era. The New Monastic Library includes reflections from new monastics as well as classic monastic resources unavailable elsewhere.

Series Editor: Jonathan Wilson-Hartgrove

Longing for
SPRING

A New
Vision for
Wesleyan
Community

ELAINE A. HEATH &
SCOTT T. KISKER

Foreword by
JONATHAN WILSON-HARTGROVE

 CASCADE *Books* · Eugene, Oregon

LONGING FOR SPRING
A New Vision for Wesleyan Community

New Monastic Library: Resources for Radical Discipleship 5

Cascade Books
An Imprint of Wipf and Stock Publishers
199 W. 8th Ave., Suite 3
Eugene, OR 97401

www.wipfandstock.com

ISBN 13: 978-1-55635-519-6

Cataloging-in-Publication data:

Heath, Elaine A., 1954–

Longing for spring : a new vision for Wesleyan community / Elaine A. Heath and Scott T. Kisker ; foreword by Jonathan Wilson-Hartgrove.

xiv + 104 p. ; 23 cm. —Includes bibliographical references.

New Monastic Library: Resources for Radical Discipleship 5

ISBN 13: 978-1-55635-519-6

1. Christian life. 2. Church. 3. Church renewal—United Methodist Church (U.S.). 4. Monastic and religious life. I. Kisker, Scott Thomas, 1967–. II. Wilson-Hartgrove, Jonathan, 1980–. III. Title. IV. Series.

BV4501.3 .H43 2010

Manufactured in the U.S.A.

For our students, and the people called Methodists

CONTENTS

ACKNOWLEDGMENTS

For all the friends, family, colleagues, and students who have helped us to think through and live toward a new day for the United Methodist Church, we give thanks. We appreciate Shellie Ross for her assistance in formatting the manuscript. Many thanks to our editors at Wipf and Stock, who have had the vision to create a series of books on new monasticism, and welcomed our contribution to that series. Elaine is deeply grateful for the generous support received from the Sam Taylor Fellowship and a Wabash Summer Research Grant to assist with research for this project.

Jonathan Wilson-Hartgrove

In the desert south of Tuscon, Arizona, just north of the U.S.–Mexico border, paved roads turn into dirt paths that wind through dried up river beds called "washes." When I was traveling those borderlands a few years ago with a group of Christian peacemakers, our guide assured us that crossing the washes would be a little bumpy, but no problem. The rivulets that wound their way over that dry ground were no challenge to our four-wheel drive. But then it started raining.

When it rains in the desert, it pours. In a matter of minutes that late summer evening, I watched tiny rivulets rise into streams that merged into one mighty river. Parched land that had been cracked before was overcome by rushing waters. In a moment, the whole landscape changed. Those of us who had witnessed it stood in awe—then quickly ran for higher ground.

My friend Diana Butler Bass says the kind of transformation I witnessed in an Arizona wash is unfolding around us in American Christianity. In her *People's History of Christianity*, Diana describes the conventional liberal/conservative divide where "two thin streams wind alongside each other between the boulders and pebbles of a great river bed, following separate ways." This is the world I was raised in. An evangelical in the Bible Belt, I struggled to find my way with Jesus quite apart from Mainline Protestants or Roman Catholics (when we talked about the Methodists at my Southern Baptist Church, we worried about their souls). On the whole, the Christian landscape felt pretty parched.

But since 1945, the river has been rising. In the latter half of the 20th century, as the last vestiges of Christendom slipped away, many Christians have found themselves caught up in a current that defies conventional wisdom. I certainly have. Trying to make sense of the Scripture verses I'd memorized in the King James Version, I got to know a Catholic sister who worked with addicts in inner-city Philadelphia. An Episcopalian professor introduced me to monastic wisdom, and I started learning from Benedictines. I ended up studying at a Methodist seminary (Lord, have mercy). The landscape is indeed changing.

Longing for Spring is a book that has grown out of Scott and Elaine's love for the people called Methodists. They are especially sensitive to the questions and longings of a new generation of their particular flock that has sat in their classrooms and come to their offices for counsel. Love compels them to be specific, and I am grateful that they have written to the church they know. I pray this book finds its way into the hands of bishops and district superintendents and annual conference members and all the other offices of Methodism that I know little to nothing about.

But this isn't just a book for Methodists. Given the rising tide we are experiencing all around us, a Baptist like myself can learn a great deal from listening in on the discernment that is happening on these pages. What the "New Methodists" want is, as a matter of fact, intimately bound up with what the new Baptists and Catholics and Quakers want. As we learn to navigate a rising tide, we are all increasingly aware of the degree to which we're in the same boat, whether we want to be or not. You might call it "Noah's ark ecumenism." Sharing a space with all God's critters ain't always easy, but it sure beats the alternative.

Because Scott and Elaine are professors of evangelism, they see clearly that riding these turbulent waters is not just about self-preservation, but rather about the good news we've been entrusted with for the sake of the whole world. We attend to the longing for spring for the sake of a world that is aching for the reconciliation of all things in Jesus Christ. If new monasticism has any gift to offer the church, I pray it is a reminder that we do well to focus our whole lives on Jesus because God has revealed in this one man the destiny of the universe. *Longing for Spring* points us in that direction.

One of my favorite images from the book of Revelation is the picture of the heavenly city, filled with the light of God, with a river of life flowing through it. The river is lined with trees that bear fruit in every season, John says, and their leaves are for the healing of the nations. Sometimes I feel like my whole life has been the result of falling into a river much wider and deeper and longer than I could have ever imagined. This great tradition that stretches back to Abraham and Eden gathers up all the tributaries of a fragmented church and, looking downstream, gathers us into something that gives life and heals divisions. In a world divided by war and economic policy, by water rights and ethnic identities, I can think of no vocation more important than joining the river that ultimately heals the nations. As we long for spring's swelling waters , may we learn to navigate them together. And may we trust our selves entirely to the God who has said he will do it.

Jonathan Wilson-Hartgrove
Series Editor
New Monastic Library: Resources for Radical Discipleship (NML)

ONE

Our Stories

INTRODUCTION

This is a book about something new that is afoot in the United Methodist Church, something holy, God-breathed, and fresh, yet grounded in the ancient ways. Like many other mainline and evangelical Christians, Methodists are beginning to ask probing questions about mission and ecclesiology. Especially among young adults we are hearing people express a desire to engage in rigorous spiritual formation coupled with a life of bi-vocational ministry. Increasing numbers of young seminarians are not planning to go into traditional ordained ministry tracks, but they are passionate about being in ministry to the poor, to disadvantaged children, to the homeless, and the like. In the manner of John and Charles Wesley, these Methodists are interested in leaving familiar confines in order to live their faith in community with those who will not come to the buildings we call "the church." They are eager to see renewal in the United Methodist Church, and willing to help bring that about. Some of these Methodists are organized into groups such as The New Methodists and the UMC Young Clergy group.[1]

---

1. The New Methodists are not to be confused with the New Methodist Conference, a group that has left the United Methodist Church and has started a new organization. The New Methodists remain committed to the UMC, but are committed to emergence and new monasticism within the denomination. See Facebook page http://www.facebook .com/home.php#/group.php?gid=9550978460. For the UMC Young Clergy group, see http://umcyoungclergy.com/.

1

This grass-roots phenomenon that is emerging around the United States has been called "the new monasticism" but really, as you shall see, it is a lot like early Methodism. In the first Appendix in this book you will find a survey of most of the recent books that cover new monasticism. For now, suffice to say that the new "monks" are women and men of all ages, married and single, some with families. They are of diverse racial, ethnic, and denominational backgrounds, and theologically left, right, and center. Rather than being identified for doctrinal commitments, they are known for a disciplined life of prayer and servanthood, especially in the "abandoned places of empire" (more about that later). Many of the new monks practice "the three R's" first articulated by John Perkins of the Christian Community Development Association (CCDA): Reconciliation, relocation, and redistribution.[2] That is, the new monks live in a stance of radical hospitality. They live and work in ways that cultivate racial reconciliation, relocation to abandoned places of empire, and redistribution of material possessions for the well being of the community. The degree of the three R's varies from one community to the next.

While most of the new monasticism has emerged outside of the United Methodist Church, increasing numbers of United Methodists are experiencing a sense of call to live and serve in this form of community. Because virtually all the emphases of the new monasticism are consistent with early Methodist vision and mission, we believe that like early Methodism, the new monasticism is a holiness movement.

Our interest in new monasticism has come from our own journeys as well as from the research, writing, and teaching we have done in our work as professors of evangelism at two United Methodist seminaries—Perkins School of Theology (Dallas, TX) and Wesley Theological Seminary (Washington, DC). We are both ordained as Elders in the United Methodist Church.

We decided to write this book in a semi-autobiographical manner, integrating some of the stories of our spiritual journeys with the narrative of monasticism, Methodism, and the rise of new monasticism in the United Methodist Church. We wrote chapters 1 and 6 together. Scott wrote chapters 2 and 3, and Elaine wrote chapters 4, 5, the appendices, and the discussion questions. Our prayer is that this little volume will

2. Christian Community Development Association, http://www.ccda.org/.

provide inspiration and hope to those who are longing for a new day for the church, and will help shape our readers' imagination toward creating dynamic new expressions of Wesleyan community.

ELAINE'S STORY

My decision began seven days after the death of my beloved friend,[3] Betty. She died on a Sunday at 7:30 in the morning. I cannot begin to tell you how much my life changed because of her. There were a thousand reasons why my life should not have amounted to anything. When I met Betty more than two decades ago, I was searching for freedom and healing, haunted with ghosts of violence from childhood. I felt my life had been hijacked, that my real self had gone underground. I hate to say it but the church had done a lot to keep me stuck. I had been indoctrinated to patriarchy, drained of life. I was like so many women in the church today whose gifts and strength are suppressed out of fear, women who are told they are proud or rebellious when they think for themselves or ask critical questions of the church, women who are told to submit to their husbands even if those husbands are violent. Then I met Betty and everything changed.

Betty was a prophet and an apostle, a church planter, a mystic, a feminist, a lover of Jesus Christ and his church. She was tall and beautiful, with high cheekbones and a broad smile that reminded me of Sophia Loren. Her large brown eyes told the story of a soul who had traveled hard roads of suffering. Compassion streamed from her heart. As Betty grew older her beauty did not fade but deepened slowly into the burnished glory of autumn. At eighty she was like the trees in Mary Oliver's poem, a pillar of translucent fire.[4]

Eventually I heard God's call to ministry because of her. Betty's love and integrity as a Christian helped me to put my hands to the plow and ask Jesus to bring the duct tape so I wouldn't change my mind. Betty taught me to pray, to believe, to take risks, to buck the system, to be equal to men, to tell the truth, to exegete the Bible, to dance for God, to enjoy good

3. In the Orthodox tradition Betty would be called my Amma, that is, my spiritual mother.

4. Oliver, "Blackwater Woods," 82.

food, to expand my horizons, to see Jesus in neighborhood kids, to hear the birds, to meditate, to rest. She taught me not to be afraid anymore. She took me by the hand and led me home to God and along the way I came home to me. She gave me Sabbath.

Betty was more Wesleyan than most Methodists I have known, although she was never a member of the United Methodist Church. What I mean is that her theology was consistent with good Wesleyan theology, with its focus on grace and holiness and the centrality of the love of God. Betty lived what we Methodists think of as the Wesleyan connection between vital piety and social justice.[5] For her evangelism was a lifestyle of mercy and prophetic courage. It was a matter of thinking, speaking, and doing the Good News while finding solidarity with the oppressed and marginalized around her.[6] She ministered to prostitutes and university professors, and everyone in between. These expressions of the love of God and neighbor were all carried out in the context of Christian community.

Over her lifetime Betty's journey had included time with Mennonites, Baptists, and Pentecostals. She had many friends among the Anglo-Catholics. Amidst all of them she was powerful in her spirituality, prayer, discernment, and Bible teaching. She was mostly evangelical according to the meaning of that label thirty years ago. But her inner freedom as a woman and her confidence in God's call were problematic to patriarchal, evangelical tribes. Like John Wesley, Betty was a person "of one book." The evangelicals liked that. They were worried, though, about Betty's love for the Christian mystics.[7] Of course the mainliners liked her a lot because of the mystics and her feminism, but the centrality of the cross in her theology was a challenge to them. The fact is that Betty was ahead of her time. She was neither liberal nor conservative. She was probably what we now call "emergent" or "missional." But she considered herself simply a Christian.

5. The truth is, Methodists don't have dibs on this blend. We just think we do, which is indicative of the whole problem I'm going to get into in this chapter.

6. I never heard her speak of Mortimer Arias, for example, but his liberating biblical theology of evangelism (Mortimer Arias, *Announcing the Reign of God*) would in many ways have resonated with Betty.

7. Wesley's Christian Library had at least eight volumes written by mystics. Madame Guyon, one of the mystics greatly admired by Wesley late in his life, was a favorite of Betty's.

At the time that I first met Betty she served on a large church staff as the pastor of counseling and discipleship. They hired her for this position because she excelled in developing small groups for spiritual formation and healing, for spiritual direction in common, and equipping leaders for this kind of work. She was sought out by people of a staggering array of religious backgrounds, both Christian and non-Christian, for spiritual counsel. She loved them all and helped many to find peace in Christ. Betty had actually been ordained by the denomination of that church, which was no small feat for a woman, but she looked at her ordination with a certain detachment, knowing that God had called her as a young girl and that she would live her call with or without the approval of an institution. She was like the Beguines that way, or Hildegard von Bingen.

Betty should have been labeled the pastor of redemption, or let's try this one, the pastor who teaches with authority and not as the scribes and Pharisees, because that is exactly what she was. For the last fifteen years of her life Betty led a small house church and helped little ragtag groups of disciples form house churches elsewhere, that she neither managed nor tried to control. She did not believe in coddling people. Somehow on a very modest income she and her husband Fred, who at one time had been a labor union organizer, traveled to other countries where they had been invited to encourage and equip house churches. On February 11, 2007, she breathed her last praise to Jesus in this life, and now she is there with Fred and the rest of the great cloud, rooting for us from the other side.

Something about Betty's death launched my decision. I took our wet bar and turned it into an altar. I know Methodists don't have bars, but our house came with one, and what are you going to do? Every morning that week I put something different on it to celebrate Betty: Trinity shaped irises to represent her life in God, an Ebenezer of stones from Lake Huron for all her answered prayers, a photo of the two of us where we are squinting into the sun on a bad hair day, a fountain with water pouring over a small white stone. I kept thinking about the river of life and the trees with healing for the nations.

In the center of the sanctified bar there was a Scripture verse that I wrote out when I told Betty about my call. I have kept it in view for daily reflection in my kitchen for the past twenty-five years since I wrote it. Betty had thrown back her head and laughed hard when I came to her after two weeks of fear and trembling and wondering if I was losing my mind, because the idea of my being called was so ridiculous. By then I knew you never knew what to expect with her, so I just waited for her to stop laughing. Wiping little tears of joy from her eyes she said, "Oh Elaine, I saw it years ago when I first met you. I saw it and wrote about it in my journal but I never told you, because you needed to hear it for yourself." That's how Betty operated. She really did "have the patience of a saint." Well, this is the text. You'll notice I took the language of the evangelical NIV translation and rather daringly changed it to be more inclusive, a bold move for me in those days.

> Therefore my dear ones, stand firm. Let nothing move you. Always give yourself fully to the work of the Lord, because you know that your labor in the Lord is not in vain. (1 Cor 15:58)

When I met Betty I barely had a high school diploma. Since those early days of friendship I went on to earn a bachelor's degree in English, an MDiv, and a PhD in theology. Today I am an elder in the United Methodist Church.[8] I have served as a pastor in four United Methodist congregations and now teach evangelism at Perkins School of Theology. Jesus really did use that duct tape. I could not have ventured forth from Betty's sheltering friendship into fifteen years of higher education and through Himalayan obstacles, if the call had not been very, very clear. Joining the United Methodist Church has been part of answering that call.

Yet there is something about the church as I have practiced it all these years that can only be described as a club. What Betty's death led me to do, is to quit the club. I do not mean I am leaving the United Methodist Church, although the thought has occurred to me at times. But there are alien priorities in our midst, anomalies that contradict the soul of our tradition. Here is one small example.

When I went to meet the pastor parish relations committee prior to being appointed to one of the churches I served, I came away with the strange knowledge that what that church wanted from their next pastor more than good preaching, pastoral care, the development of children's ministry or just someone who could write a decent bulletin, was a pastor

---

8. In the United Methodist Church, for readers unfamiliar with our polity, an elder is a minister who is ordained to "word and sacrament," to serve as a pastor of a church. A great deal of preparation is required for one to become an elder.

who would live in their parsonage. That was really and truly their top priority. The last pastor, for a number of reasons hadn't been able to live in the parsonage. If a pastor would live in the parsonage, they reasoned, giving would increase, the kids who had graduated from high school and left church would come back, and everyone would contribute more stuff to the annual rummage sale. Life would be good. All manner of thing would be well. I left the meeting and wondered what I was getting myself into.[9]

Yes, I have thought about leaving the mother ship. But despite these little anomalies that are everywhere in the United Methodist Church, I have to tell you, she has welcomed me with open arms in her own way, just as Betty did, and it is God's call that led me into the United Methodist Church and that keeps me here. Like George Matheson says, "O Love that will not let me go."[10] The love of God is in my heart for "the people called Methodists."[11]

The thing is, about a year into seminary it all began to converge. I realized one day with some surprise, that my closest friends in seminary were almost all Methodists. Not only that, but it occurred to me that the theology and spirituality Betty had imparted to me was deeply consistent with what I was finding out about Wesley and his vision for spreading scriptural holiness across the land. Like a locomotive gathering speed on a downhill grade I remembered the clarity of call God had given me years before in which I saw myself working in a mainline setting,[12] the prayer and missional DNA Betty had given me, and the freedom for women to pursue ordination in the United Methodist Church. The more I found out about Wesleyan theology and history, the more convinced I became that

9. As it turned out, once we got acquainted they allowed that it would be nice to have a men's ministry, and a few other contributions from me that were related to my theology degree, and we were able to work together to develop some wonderful ministries in that little church. I learned much from them along the way, and thank God for the gift of serving as their pastor.

10. Matheson, "O Love That Wilt Not Let Me Go," 480.

11. When I first began spending time with Methodism I noticed this phrase popping up everywhere. It seemed odd to me, one of those churchy phrases we use that "outsiders" find amusing. We never say, for example, "the people called Nebraskans." I learned in time that the phrase went back to the early days of Methodism and John Wesley, when they were beginning to define their rule of life.

12. That in itself was pretty crazy, given the fact that I had always been in an evangelical environment. But God had clearly shown me I was going somewhere that would be in a mainline context.

I was a closet Methodist.[13] So I came out. I joined the United Methodist Church.

I am among the people called Methodists for the long haul. In the United Methodist Church I found the community of saints who would help me to answer both the ordination side of my call and the academic side. Their people have become my people, their God is my God. Whither they goest I must go, even if I make noise along the way. My hand is taped to the plow. This is the field Jesus picked for me. They will have to throw me out to get me out.

So here I am now, working at Perkins School of Theology with terrific students who are preparing for ministry. I have the best colleagues a person could hope for, who help me grow out of my little confinements day by day. Sometimes I look at my bank statement and can't believe I get a paycheck for doing what makes me fully alive. (Don't tell the payroll people I said that, because I don't want them to get any ideas.) There is nothing more exhilarating than equipping God's saints for the mission. And that is why I have to leave the club. I have to do this for my students and for the people called Methodists. As my Texan friends say, I have to do it for y'all.

I have been teaching now for several years and there is scarcely a week that passes without at least one student, former student or pastor confiding to me that she or he is thinking of leaving the church. Not God, not ministry, not vocation, just the denomination. The mother ship. I have watched them leave, with sorrow, as they tried to find a place where they could more fully live their call. They have gone to the non-denominational churches, the Orthodox church, the Baptists, the Pentecostals, the Episcopalians, the Free Methodists, the Unitarians, the Disciples of Christ. Some have left the institutional church and are doing other things, with varying degrees of success. Some have stayed with us and labor on, hindered and suffocated, dwindling down and wondering what they should do next. They always ask me to tell them why they should stay with us,

13. One of the things I love about Wesleyan theology at its best is its ecumenism. Being a Methodist means in many ways, simply being a Christian. Methodism, rightly understood, is a holiness movement, a way of life that is supposed to bring renewal to the "one holy, catholic, apostolic church." In fact Ted Campbell writes that "we should fervently pray for the day when Methodism ceases to exist" because the church has been renewed and Methodism is no longer necessary (Campbell, *Methodist Doctrine*, 31).

stay in the system. Me, of all people, devoted friend and student of Betty Whose Faith Was Larger than Institutions and A Threat to the Status Quo. They are asking me what to do.

Meanwhile reports are coming out from Wesley Seminary that we have an alarming decline in the number of clergy under the age of thirty-five, and in our good methodical way we have charted the bad news. During the past twenty years the number of ordained elders under the age of thirty-five has taken a nosedive from 3,219 to 850.[14] On top of these reports are other reports about the stagnation of the church, the decline of the church, the closing of churches, financial crises, and so on. Those little anomalies are not so little. We are in a full-blown institutional crisis. Is this a bad thing? I don't think so.

Because what we now have on our hands is primordial soup. It is time for some new life forms to crawl out and gasp on the quivering beach. It is a new day. God is behind this. This is one of those God acts that we blame on the devil. And now I can finally tell you about the club.

It is the club of Denominationalism Posing as the Church. Denominationalism is dead. Self-serving institutionalism is dead. The notion that the church is a bureaucracy that should look and act like the federal government of the United States is dead. That which John Wesley greatly feared has come upon us.[15]

Denominationalism worked once upon a time. And let's be honest, some form of institution is necessary for the church to function as a community. But the institution that serves itself, as Walter Wink helps us understand, is in collusion with the powers and principalities.[16] In the real world we are hoping to reach with the good news of Jesus, more than 80 percent of people ages sixteen to twenty-nine have a negative view of Christianity,[17] and the church as club is a major reason for that statistic. We are in a post-denominational world, one in which the institutionally self-serving ways of Christendom are crumbling and all the privileged,

14. Weems, "Are Young Elders Disappearing?" 6–7.

15. Wesley claimed that he did not fear Methodism would ever cease to exist, but that Methodism would become a "dead sect," a form of religion without the power of the Holy Spirit.

16. For an introduction to Wink's theology of the powers and how they influence churches and other institutions, see Walter Wink, *Powers That Be.*

17. Kinnaman and Lyons, *Unchristian*, 25–27.

consumeristic, colonizing assumptions of the church are falling apart. We are in a new day in which the church is moving to the margins, a time that calls us to repent of our jockeying for power and privilege in a secular culture. It is time for denominations, including the United Methodist Church, to move with the Holy Spirit and become a kenotic church.

To use the language of mystical theology, it is time for Methodism to return to holiness, to practice *ecstasis*, going *out of* ourselves. It is about becoming a literalist in practicing love of God *and neighbor*. Something about Betty's death opened my eyes to see my actual neighbors, and to realize with astonishment that God has deployed me, a pastor and theologian, to *this* neighborhood with *these* neighbors, and *our* schools. How could I not have realized this sooner? It is so painfully and blatantly obvious, and here I am with enough college degrees to paper one wall, and I did not see it. The neighborhood, not the big brick building with a cross and flame, is where we Christians are sent to be the church. The neighborhood is my parish, whether my neighbors become Methodists or not. What matters is that they experience the kingdom of God coming near, and that they know it is a kingdom of love.[18]

I can hear mental brakes screeching as I type these words. "Wait a minute!" Someone is saying, "I thought you said you weren't going to leave the United Methodist Church? I thought you said you were stuck like gum on our Methodist shoe?" Like Lucy, I have some 'splaining to do.

And that is what this book is about. Along with several other professors of evangelism, Scott and I were at Lake Junaluska for a conference. During an afternoon break we were talking about our experiences with students and pastors who are eyeing the open water while they ask us for one good reason to stay on the ship. Around and around the Lake we walked, talking and pondering. Being academic types, our first impulse was to study the problem to death. But we both knew that God had something else in mind, beyond our research and writing. We knew that God was calling us to live into a new life form, a Methodist life form that is true to our heritage *and* our post-denominational context. We parted ways agreeing to think about it some more, and pray about working on a book together. But there were still pieces missing, at least for me.

18. Luke 10:1–9.

Then Betty died. And something opened in me, a vast inner space that was like the Texas hill country, wild and free, covered with bluebonnets. A wind began to blow in my soul, warm and scented with spring. Something lifted film-like from my vision so I could see from a new perspective. I saw myself and my years in the church, my efforts with the club, the goodness of my desire for the club to recover, and the futility of it. I saw the mercy of God and the simplicity of the way. I saw resurrection. I saw how to live in the neighborhood as my parish, and I welcomed the kingdom of God. I had been set free.

My epiphany seems rather modest compared to that of John Wesley, who declared that *the world* was his parish. What did he mean by that? He continued to be an Anglican clergyman and to worship in the Anglican Church after the Methodist movement began. It was not about who were formal members in the Anglican Church, but about seeing his field for ministry in a new way that staggered his imagination. He saw that it was to the world, not just to a small group of Anglicans, that he had been deployed.

✓ In this book Scott and I are exploring what it means to live in the neighborhood as our parish. We are looking at the new monasticism for Methodists in a post-denominational world. We do this out of our deep love and commitment to our students and to the people called Methodists. It is our dream to spark the imagination of the United Methodist Church to see and embrace the new life forms that are emerging, the kind of life forms that are, when you trace them down to their roots, utterly Wesleyan.

SCOTT'S STORY

Elaine and I started out in different wings of the Methodist movement. She began her spiritual journey in an "evangelicalized" branch of holiness Methodism. I was raised in the elite version of "mainline" Methodism. Over time, our experiences of God's Spirit have shown each of us sides of God's character that moved us closer to one another. And we both sense something is terribly wrong with contemporary United Methodism.

Technically I am not a cradle United Methodist (I was baptized in a Presbyterian Church). But when I was five years old my family moved to another city and we became Methodist. My father had been raised Presbyterian and my mother Methodist. So, as good Americans, we checked out both and chose First United Methodist Church, a tall steeple church near the public university campus where my father worked.

Some of the struggles Elaine faced as she answered God's call were simply not a part of my world. The local church I grew up in certainly had no issues with women's ordination. On that, and any number of social issues, the preaching and preachers I remember were classically and optimistically liberal. The sermons I heard were opposed to nuclear weapons, and supportive of the United Nations and America's "great society." My church knew it was secure, as most of the mainline churches did. We were secure in our place and status within the community, secure in our beautiful stone building on the corner, secure in our ability to fill the pews on Sunday (even the balcony), secure that the next generation would grow up to be good liberal church-going Methodists.

Despite the full sanctuary there was something barren about the community. It wasn't making new children of God. That started to be clear to me during confirmation. I went through the formalities, but was not touched spiritually. No one else was either, as far as I could tell. When the classes were over, my only question was whether "joining the church" meant that I had to be a member of *this* church for the rest of my life. My question should have demonstrated my fundamental misunderstanding of "church," that it was no more than a social organization which I joined and could un-join. No one corrected my ecclesiology. The answer was simply "no." So I figured, "Why not, it'll make my parents happy," and I was "confirmed."

Gradually, many of my class of confirmands simply dropped out. The institution kept humming. But the rhetoric of church life seemed less and less connected to reality, at least to mine. One of the things rarely talked about in our church (except on a grand social scale which left me out personally) was sin. I don't remember ever hearing about the need for a new life, about the power of the resurrection to "save me." The de facto anthropology of our church didn't presuppose the fall of humanity. We humans could make the world and ourselves better. Going through puberty, sin was the one reality I knew existed. I knew subconsciously I needed saving. But church on Sunday morning did not give me a language to talk about that, make judgments about it, or deal with it in my own life.

Fortunately our youth group was run by some radically Christian college students. They pursued me and communicated to me the reality of the world, and of Christ and His kingdom, in a way that connected with my life. It took a while, but their witness and my wrestling eventually resulted in my wanting to commit my life to Christ. Whatever the disappointments I have with United Methodism, I owe the fact that I am a Christian to a United Methodist youth group. So when I went to college and joined the chapter of InterVarsity, I always attended the local United Methodist Church on Sunday mornings. [19] When I sensed a call to attend seminary, I chose a United Methodist Divinity School.

At seminary, I "discovered" John Wesley. I was shocked to find out that he had had a religious experience similar to my own. I couldn't remember Aldersgate ever being talked about in any of the Methodist churches I had attended. I devoured his sermons. Reading them during my job at the circulation desk in the University Library, I brainwashed myself theologically. I found in Wesley and historic Methodism a glimpse of the kind of Christian community I was looking for—a spiritual depth only possible through relationships and mutual discipline, the sacred boundaries of mutual accountability. That glimpse has given me hope. It is why I am United Methodist. I know enough about Wesley and the movement to know that the kingdom of God did not come in its fullness in the eighteenth century. Yet eighteenth century Methodists certainly seemed more earnest about seeking it first, and the power of the kingdom certainly seemed more evident in their midst. Can it happen again?

The problem that faces the contemporary "liberal" and "conservative" church, not just United Methodism, is a spiritual coldness that is visible to its members and to the world. This state of the church is nothing new. It has occurred repeatedly throughout the history of God's people. John Wesley named this phenomenon in his sermon, "The Causes of the Inefficacy of Christianity." The wealthier we become, the more successful we seem, the more comfortable in the society we feel, the less we depend on the Trinity for our daily bread, and the less willing we are to live according to the norms and strictures of scriptural holiness. Church becomes

19. While in college I was given a copy of David Lowes Watson's, *Early Methodist Class Meeting*. That was the first I had heard of class meetings. Until then I had no idea Methodism had something to say about discipleship.

another organization. We begin playing church according to rules of the world's games.

Back in the early 1980s a movie called *War Games* starred a very young Matthew Broderick. In the movie a computer designed to simulate nuclear warfare decided to take matters into its own hands and launch an attack on the Soviet Union. Broderick's character, by making the computer play itself in tic-tac-toe, taught the computer that, like tic-tac-toe, thermonuclear war couldn't be won. The moral of the movie: "The only way to win, is not to play the game."

The history of renewal always involves a rejection of the world's games. The church is renewed when it regrasps what it means to be church—not defined (first and foremost) by its clergy or hierarchy, but by a community shaped by the Trinity—a place of care and accountability. When what calls itself "church" does not embody this, for whatever reasons, Christians (motivated, we believe, by the Holy Spirit) have sought to gather together in various forms of community to incarnate it. These monastics, by making the kingdom a visible reality, have renewed the church. This is what Elaine and I hope: that this book will inspire ordinary Methodists to engage the new monasticism in a variety of forms.

TWO

Early Stories of Intentional Community and Church Renewal

The expansion of Christianity in the Roman Empire prior to the Constantinian era was quite amazing. It was not due to strategic wielding of social influence or clever marketing. In the letter to Diogenes, written around AD 200, a writer described these peculiar people to a Roman official.

> Christians are not distinguished from the rest of humankind either in locality or in speech or in customs. For they dwell not somewhere in cities of their own, neither do they use some different language, nor practice an extraordinary kind of life . . . While they dwell in cities of Greeks and barbarians . . . and follow the native custom in dress and food and the other arrangements of life, yet the constitution of their own citizenship, which they set forth is marvelous, and confessedly contradicts expectation. They dwell in their own countries, but only as sojourners . . . Every foreign country is a fatherland to them, and every fatherland is foreign . . . They find themselves in the flesh and yet they live not after the flesh. Their existence is on earth, but their citizenship is in heaven. They obey the established laws, and they surpass the laws in their own lives . . . War is waged against them as aliens by the Jews and persecution is carried on against them by the Greeks, and yet those who hate them cannot tell the reason for their hostility. In a word, what the soul is in the body, this the Christians are in the world . . . [they] are kept in the world as in a prison house, and yet they themselves hold the world together.[1]

1. Bosch, *Transforming Mission*, 211.

Christianity, at times illegal and semi-covert, by "surpassing the law in their own lives" spread to every corner of the Empire. It was not a majority religion by any means, but it crossed all sorts of boundaries, cultures, and local religious cults.

In 312 a competitor for the highest office in the land had a vision of the cross (and probably also of the power of this movement to advance his own political ambitions).[2] This vision and several military victories got him into power. Constantine made Christianity legal in 313. This was not a bad thing, but the approval of the Emperor changed the character of the church in ways that it could not have foreseen. It turned the call of discipleship on its head. It became commonplace and socially advantageous to be a Christian. Discipline lagged. The church began playing the world's game.[3]

John Wesley has an interesting quote about this change in the fortunes of the Christian religion and Constantine's conversion. He wrote of Constantine:

> I say [he] "called himself a Christian" for I dare not affirm that
> *he was one* . . . For surely there never was a time wherein Satan
> gained so fatal an advantage over the church of Christ as when
> such a flood of riches, and honour, and power broke in upon it,
> particularly the clergy.[4]

Wesley's comment about the clergy is very relevant. The change in the character of Christianity brought about numerical growth, but not the healthy reproduction of disciples. Like the growth of mainline Christianity after World War II, and of evangelicalism in the 1980s, numerical growth masked the true condition of the church. Yet the fourth century situation brought forth the first experiments in communal Christian holy living. Those experiments began with laypeople.

---

2. Constantine had a history of visions that advanced his political ambitions. In a 310 speech he claimed to have seen a vision of Apollo and Victory presenting him with laurel wreaths. He quoted the poet Virgil who had foretold of a saving figure who would be given "rule of the whole world." Constantine appropriated the prophesy to himself.

3. The triumphalism of Eusebius's *Ecclesiasical History* demonstrates that the interests of the Empire and the interests of the church became difficult to separate, even for pious Christians.

4. Wesley, "Signs of the Times," 529.

When we think of monasticism, we often think of the late medieval version, which was dominated by the clergy, integrated into society, and possessed of huge amounts of wealth. That is not how monastic experiments began. Most monks were lay people who responded to the perceived distance between the call of Jesus and the lack of a disciplined holy community in the church they experienced. Clergy did not lead these movements of reform.

The term laity comes from the Greek word *laos,* which simply means "the people." The laity are the people of God. The word clergy comes from the Greek word *kleros,* which means "lot," or "that which is chosen by lot." You may remember in the book of Acts, Matthias was chosen by lot from among the people to fill the apostolic position left vacant by Judas Iscariot.[5] In other words, the clergy are the laity who have drawn the short stick. What the history of monasticism makes clear is that any renewal will come from "the people" of God.

Monasticism began with individual lay Christians retreating from society to deserted places to pursue holiness. The famous Saint Anthony, who is credited with creating monasticism, was a layperson who desired to pursue a higher Christian life, gave away his possessions, and went to live alone in the wilderness.[6] Gradually a group of other seekers gathered to live near him.

The first true monastic communities were organized within a decade of Christianity's legalization by the Emperor—sometime between AD 318 and 323. They were the work of another layperson named Pachomius. Pachomius had been converted while he was in the Roman army. He had been pressed into military service against his will and local Christians ministered to him and his fellow captives. This practical evangelism paid off. When he got out of the army (without having had to fight), he converted and was baptized around 313.[7]

His desire to pursue holiness led him to try to live as an ascetic near St. Anthony, initially mentored by another ascetic name Palamon.[8] When Palamon died, others gathered around Pachomius, seeking to learn from

5. Acts 1:12–26.
6. Athanasius, *Life of St. Anthony,* 31. See also Harmless, *Desert Christians,* 60–74.
7. Veilleaux, *Life of Pachomius,* 27–28.
8. Ibid., 40.

him. Once they numbered one hundred monks, he built a church for them, which became the center of this community of ascetics. He eventually founded eight other communities where laymen or women, with male and female lay leadership, experimented with Christian community. Pachomius "did not want any clerics in his monasteries for fear of jealousy and vainglory."[9] He is also credited with establishing the first "Rule of Life" to guide and discipline these lay communities.[10]

DARK AGES RENEWAL: BENEDICT'S COMMUNITIES

Even St. Benedict, whose "Rule" for monastic living guided intentional Christian experiments for generations, was a layperson. He was never ordained. Those who lived in the communities he oversaw were lay people. In fact, he never intended to found an "order" in the sense we think of it, today.

The church in Benedict's day was engaged in the doctrinal disputes between the East and West, which would eventually result in schism. These disputes manifested themselves in the games of the church hierarchy. In 498 two different popes were elected after the death of Pope Anastasius II. Symmachus (considered by the Roman Catholic Church to be legitimate) was chosen by part of the clergy and approved by part of the Roman senate. The same day another group of clergy, friendly to Eastern concerns and supported by part of the Senate, met and elected Laurentius as pope. For the next fifteen years, these two "popes," and their supporters, engaged in a contentious, and often violent, dispute that divided the church until 514.

Benedict lived in Rome when all this was going on. He was completing his studies in rhetoric and law and probably looking forward to a lucrative career, which would continue (what we would consider) the upper middle class style of life in which he had been raised. Although we do not know exactly why, Benedict decided to leave off his studies and leave Rome around AD 500. The main source of information on Benedict's life was written around 593 by Pope Gregory the Great who wrote that he "rejected the study of literature and left his home and his father's affairs. His

9. Ibid., 47–48.
10. Harmless, *Desert Christians*, 124–30.

sole desire was to find favor with God, and so he made the religious life his goal. He withdrew then, knowingly ignorant and wisely unlearned."[11] Benedict traveled to a village about forty miles from Rome and joined a group of like-minded seekers living in community there.

In retreat from the world he prayed and studied and gained a reputation for holiness. After he was reputed to have performed a miracle, the attention from townspeople grew too great. He left that community and went to another small community living on the mountain of Subiaco. While there his reputation for holiness and discipline spread and a third community asked him to come and lead them. This did not go well. Reportedly his new community tried to poison him. He returned to Subiaco, perhaps a bit chastened.

At Subiaco others, who were seeking holiness and were dissatisfied with the ordinary life of the church, began to seek him out. Eventually there were twelve different communities in the valley. Each consisted of its own superior and twelve members.[12] Benedict oversaw them all, and they gradually developed a pattern of life that would serve as a model— one where work and prayer and study were all sacred activities to be held in balance. The Rule of St. Benedict was not written for clergy but for lay people who want to live in obedience to Christ. It was intended as a practical guide for holy community in the midst of a rebellious world.

> Listen my son, and turn the ear of thine heart to the precepts of thy Master. Receive readily, and faithfully carry out the advice of a loving Father, so that by the work of obedience you may return to Him, whom you have left by the sloth of disobedience. For thee, therefore, whosoever thou be, my words are intended, who, giving up thy own will, dost take the all-powerful and excellent arms of obedience to fight under the Lord Christ, the true King.[13]

Benedict died around 547. However, the communities following his rule of discipleship continued to spread northward and, in what we think of as the Dark Ages, were perhaps the most powerful tool for spreading the Gospel in what was then pagan Europe. In a brutal world, their evan-

---

11. Gregory the Great, *Dialogues of Gregory*, 3.

12. These seem much like a Methodist class meeting, each with its class leader and no more than twelve members.

13. Benedict of Nursia, *Rule of St. Benedict*, 1.

gelism was accomplished, not through coercion, but through the creation of communities of devoted lay people, striving to live a holistic and holy life of body, mind, and spirit. Today there are plenty of seekers looking for a model for creating down-to-earth yet spiritual expressions of community. What is needed are multiple examples of how to do it.

FORMS OF COMMUNITY IN THE MIDDLE AGES: THE BEGUINES AND THE BRETHREN OF THE COMMON LIFE

Five hundred years later, lay people were continuing to find creative ways to live out God's kingdom. The twelfth and thirteenth centuries were again times of great turmoil in society and church, especially for devoted Christian women. Marriage was not always an option. Men were scarce. The Crusades had removed quite a few and the Second Lateran Council (AD 1139) finally made it absolutely clear that married men may not enter the priesthood in the western church. Monasticism was not always attractive. Benedictine monasticism had come to mean an isolated cloistered life away from interaction with the world. Not all Christian women sensed a call to permanently renounce marriage. So women began to create their own options of faithful Christian community.

In the mid-1100s small groups of women in what is now Belgium began to live together at the edge of cities and towns.[14] They lived communally, and committed their lives to prayer and service to the poor, but they differed from the pattern that had come to define monasticism. Each community was autonomous. Each made its own "Rule" to guide communal life and enhance simplicity. Members did not take permanent vows of poverty, retaining ownership of property. They were not cloistered. Those who joined often worked in the town to support themselves and not burden the community. Neither did they take permanent vows of celibacy. Women could come into the community having been married (some even with children) and could leave the community to marry.

14. Bowie, "Introduction," 14–15. A Beguine movement began in Fiona in the diocese of Liège in Brabant. A group of women, who had been associated with a priest named Lambert le Begue in Liege who encouraged them to "live religiously," and who were later recognized as Beguines, appeared between 1170 and 1175. See also McDonnell, *Beguines and Beghards*, 7.

The women came to be known as Beguines, probably related to the word for "beg," referring to their petitions to God. By the middle of the 1200s they had spread throughout what is now Belgium, the Netherlands, and parts of Germany. Some of them, like the Beguinage of Ghent were as large as a town.[15]

They came to be known both for their service and their mystical spirituality, which emphasized the humanity of Christ and devotion to the sacrament. At the time, the laity rarely received communion. When even traditional religious orders might celebrate the Eucharist only three times a year, Beguine communities took communion weekly or more frequently. Several Beguine women wrote and published mystical works of piety in the language of the people (rather then Latin) focused on divine love.[16] Some even took up preaching.[17] These activities did not endear them to the clerical hierarchy. But their lived piety came to define the character of Christianity experienced by the average person.

I want to jump ahead another hundred years to the mid-1300s. The church was again caught up in the games of the world and facing schism. For roughly seventy years the French controlled the papacy and the pope was resident in Avignon, France. Then in 1378, two popes were elected, an Italian in Rome, a Frenchman in Avignon. Different factions of the church throughout Europe allied themselves with one or the other of these popes, often for ethnic and political reasons. The situation got so convoluted that at one point there were three people claiming to be the legitimate pope, which was not finally resolved until the Council of Constance in 1417.[18]

In the midst of this disorder a semi-monastic movement began which had tremendous impact on late medieval Christianity. Gerhardt Groote (1340–1384) was raised in what is now the Netherlands, where the Beguines had been strong. He was the son of wealthy merchants, well educated, and intended to be a scholar. At twenty-six, he traveled to Avignon, to the papal court. Though he was not ordained, the trip secured for him a cannonry (actually two) at the cathedrals of Utrecht and Aachen. These provided him with a sizeable stipend and his life as a well-provided-for

15. McDonnell, *Beguines and Beghards*, 479.

16. Bowie, *Beguine Spirituality*, 40–42.

17. McDonnell, *Beguines and Beghards*, 343, 412.

18. The council of Constance was also where the Czech reformer Jan Huss was executed, setting the stage for the fracturing of the western church 100 years later.

scholar seemed secure. He was also noted for his debauchery and dabbling in astrology.[19]

In 1374, after recovering from a deadly illness, Groote had a conversion experience. He then wrote "our resolutions and intentions, but not vows," to guide his new life.[20] After about two years, he went to live at a Carthusian monastery, but did not take monastic vows. Instead, sometime after the elections of competing popes, he renounced his positions, distributed all his worldly possessions, and became an itinerant lay preacher throughout the diocese of Utrecht.[21]

His preaching was uninhibited. He called all people, lay and clergy, to repentance and a holy life. None of this made him popular, especially with the clergy. They did not appreciate his accusations or the disruptions to their parishes. Eventually they brought charges of heterodoxy against him. Groote issued a public protest, declaring that he had simply preached Jesus, and would submit to the judgment of the church. The bishop issued an edict that prohibited all lay people from preaching, which should have silenced his ministry. Even so, Groote apparently continued to preach through the last year of his life. He died of the plague in 1384.[22]

The results of his preaching were that some were convicted and a small band of followers (mostly lay, but some clergy) became the first group of what came to be known as the "Brethren of the Common Life." Like the Beguines, those who heeded his call to repentance did not leave the world to join a typical cloistered monastery. Instead, they remained in their vocations, whether clergy or lay, and sought to live out the call to Christ-like living in the world. They met together for mutual support, cultivation of their spiritual lives and service. Their focus became the education of the poor.[23]

The impact of the Brethren of the Common Life and their witness for holy living in the world was profound. Out of these associations developed a system of free schools, the first experiment with broadly available education in Europe. Some of the finest minds of the late middle ages

19. Van Engen, "Introduction," 36–38.

20. Ibid., 65–75.

21. Ibid., 37.

22. Van Zijl, *Gerard Groote.*

23. Van Engen, *Devotio Moderna,* 12–37.

were educated in these schools, and some of the greatest spiritual teachers were nurtured. Thomas à Kempis, who wrote what is today still a classic of Christian spirituality, *The Imitation of Christ,* was a member of the Brethren of the Common Life.

Conclusion

These historical expressions of lay Christian community illustrate a pattern of renewal. Some come from the center of what monasticism has meant and some might seem peripheral. All convey that time and again the church (the "people/laity of God") is renewed when members of the body begin to live out examples of simple faithfulness that can be seen and imitated by the world around it. Often the "church" is judged by what happens at the level of clergy, councils and conferences. Too often the politics look little different from the world. We see the game, the endless rounds of ecclesial tic-tac-toe. Even Christians get disillusioned and become cynical. And the devil gains ground. Throughout Methodism and the larger church, God's people are finding different and creative ways to follow Christ corporately and visibly, in the world as it is. God's people don't need to wait for permission to be obedient. The history of renewal can repeat itself again. God can do, and is doing, surprising things. "The only way to win is not to play the game."

THREE

Protestant Models of Intentional Community

The Protestant Reformation was, at least outwardly, a disaster for monasticism. To be fair to the reformers, monasticism in the late middle ages was
hardly an example of radical commitment to seeking first the kingdom
of God. Though monks technically took vows of poverty, chastity, and
obedience, monasteries were rich. They had become an acceptable alternative for the second sons and illegitimate children of the nobility—places
where they could live in comfort (thanks to pious donations from family
members). Ambition could be channeled into ecclesial rather than secular
politics. Monasticism had become another example of "the game." The
multiple attempts at monastic reform in the fifteenth century (by people
like Theresa of Avila) point to wider problems of lax discipline and complacency. Martin Luther began his spiritual journey among the reformed
Augustinian monks.

Where the Reformation was adopted, most monastic institutions
had few defenders among ordinary Christians. The chorus to a song sung
by German peasants in the sixteenth-century peasant rebellion translates
roughly, "Spears forward, up and over, set fire to the roof of the cloister." In
Protestant Germany and Switzerland, where monasteries were disbanded
(sometimes voluntarily), their revenue was often appropriated to support
social services, free schools, or to assist the poor. Not all reformers were
so pious. In England, Henry VIII simply appropriated the monasteries'
wealth and property for himself or his supporters. Yet even where older
monastic traditions were swept away by new reforms, the impulse toward
intentional Christian community remained.

THE REFORMERS

The earliest example of this impulse occurred within a decade of the beginning of the Reformation in Switzerland. A group of younger followers of Ulrich Zwingli (1484–1531) the reformer of Zurich became disillusioned by the way city politics was allowed to dictate the pace of reform. For these unrealistic "radicals," some of whose fathers were Councilmen, being a Christian meant a level of holiness and discipline that bourgeois civil leaders would never countenance. Christians, they believed, transferred their citizenship from the world's kingdom to Christ's kingdom, and no longer played the world's games.

What this group became best know for is the practice of believer's baptism, which earned them the label Anabaptists or "rebaptizers" by their detractors. Originally a secondary issue, this return to the pre-Constantinian norm of church practice was an extension of their convictions about the separation of God's church from State authorities. Entering Christ's church could not be coerced, even of infants. True Christian commitment, they believed, meant choosing a disciplined holy life in community, similar in many ways to monasticism.

A "confession," composed by a secret gathering of Anabaptists in the town of Schleitheim, chaired by a former monk named Michael Sattler (1490–1527) became a sort of "rule of life" for Anabaptist communities. The Schleitheim Confession listed seven characteristics including a commitment to renounce violence and to submit to the discipline of the community under the leadership of a pastor.[1] Anabaptist meetings were, by necessity, small, gathering secretly in houses and barns. They identified with the poor, because they were, by and large, the poor. Many came from peasant stock and those who did not had their means of financial gain severely curtailed because of their convictions. Where they were able to form communities, several adopted common ownership of property.[2]

Their commitment to a more radical expression of Christianity did not endear them to their more mainstream neighbors. Despite similarities to monastic discipline, the punishment for refusing to give up these radical practices was death in Protestant and Roman Catholic territories.

1. Estep, *Anabaptist Story*, 57–73.
2. Ibid., 127–49.

Of the initial group in Zurich, all were executed or died in prison within a few years of being baptized.[3] Even showing an excess of piety (as determined by your neighbors) could get you accused of being an Anabaptist, whether or not you had received believer's baptism. Yet the movement was incredibly influential.

They influenced one mainstream reformer, whose experiments in intentional community became a model for Protestantism generally. Martin Bucer (1491–1551), like Martin Luther and Sattler, had been a monk before he was won over to the Reformation. While studying theology in Heidelberg, he heard Luther defend himself and his critique of indulgence selling. For a while Bucer considered himself one of Luther's disciples. After receiving his Bachelor of Theology, he petitioned to be released from his monastic vows (which was granted) and, while serving as a priest in Landstuhl, he married a former nun, Elizabeth Silbereisen (d.1541). This and teaching "Luther's heresy" eventually got him excommunicated.

In 1523, at the age of thirty-one and with few safe options, Bucer arrived in Strasbourg, a free city open to reforming ideas. Married and excommunicated, the council would not allow him to preach. He wrote Zwingli hoping for a position but received no reply. Desperate, he began to lecture to small groups in a private home. That same year, he published the content of his teaching in a pamphlet entitled, roughly translated, "No one should live for himself but for others, and how one may attain this."[4]

Eventually, Bucer became one of the leading reformers in Strasbourg. There, a number of Anabaptists found relative security for a time, and Bucer began to take seriously some of their critiques of church.[5] During his last years in Strasbourg, Bucer established *christlichen Gemeinschaften* ("Christian fellowships") within the authorized church. These were small groups of devout persons who voluntarily gathered together and pledged to submit to mutual discipline and live according to the law of love. Like monastic communities had been, these groups were intentional lay communities within the larger church.[6]

---

3. Ibid, 29–55.
4. Bucer, *Instruction in Christian Love.*
5. Oyer, "Bucer Opposes the Anabaptists," 24–50.
6. Burnett, *Yoke of Christ.*

THE QUEST FOR ORTHODOXY

This concern for lay spirituality was at the core of the Reformation impulse. Luther's ninety-five theses stemmed from pastoral concern for the parishioners in Wittenberg. Selling indulgences undermined church teaching on repentance and holy living, as well as the legitimacy and authority of the church. However, Reformation debates rather quickly came to focus on doctrine (What should Christians believe?) rather than on discipleship (How should Christians live?). On that, even Protestants couldn't agree.

At the Diet of Augsburg (1530), Bucer joined with moderate Lutheran Phillip Melanchthon (1497–1560) to try and mediate the dispute between Protestants over the nature of Christ's presence in the Lord's Supper. It didn't work. Bucer participated again with Melanchthon and Roman Catholic Cardinal Contrarini (himself a member of the semi-monastic Order of Divine Love) at the Colloquy of Ratisbon (1541). The colloquy, (Reformed, Lutheran, and Roman Catholic together) hammered out a joint statement on justification by faith. But by then the constituencies they represented were too resistant and the agreement was not ratified.

This tendency to define Christianity by adherence to doctrinal statements intensified in the latter part of the 1500s. The next generation of Roman, Lutheran, and Reformed systematic theologians worked to perfect and protect the doctrines that divided them within systematic statements. The reforming Council of Trent (1545–1563) established the norms for Roman Catholic doctrine and worship, which specifically excluded Lutherans, Calvinists, and Anabaptists. The Formula of Concord (1577) was the Lutheran answer to Trent. With precise and emphatic language, it defined Lutheran orthodoxy, over against Calvinists, Catholics, and Anabaptists. Even moderate Lutheran positions (held by the followers of Luther's friend and successor Phillip Melanchthon) were excluded as too Calvinist or too Roman.

Finally, the Synod of Dordt (1618–1619) was convened by the Dutch parliament in the midst of their war for independence to defend orthodox Calvinism. Their conclusions were drawn up to exclude the teachings of Jacob Arminius (who had recently died), whose followers asserted that God's grace enabled humans to cooperate with grace, that election was according to God's foreknowledge of who would believe, that Christ died for all people, that grace could be resisted, and that people could truly believe and still fall away. These points seemed too close to Roman or Anabaptist positions. They were condemned.

There is a joke about Christian doctrinal unity that goes like this: A man walking across a bridge sees another man about to jump off. Being a Christian he rushes to convince the man that his life is worth living. Through their conversation he discovers that the potential suicide victim is also Christian. "Oh, really, that is great. You can't end your life. Christ died for it." He begins asking the jumper questions to keep him occupied. "Are you Protestant or Catholic?" "You're a Protestant, that's great, I am Protestant, too. So you know salvation is all by grace." "Are you a Calvinist or Arminian?" "You're Arminian, that is great, I'm Arminian, too. So you know God loves everyone, including you. Do you believe in infant or adult baptism?" "You believe in infant baptism, that's great. Me, too. So you know that God's grace comes before we can do anything." "Do you believe authority comes through bishops, elders, or the congregation?" "Bishops!?". . . "Oh" . . . "Heretic!" And he pushes him off the bridge.

One of the dangers present with the doctrinal divisions within the various reformations was that most of the divisions had armies. As the Calvinists were constructing their orthodoxy at Dort, war broke out in Bohemia (now the Czech Republic) between the Catholic Holy Roman Emperor and Reformed Frederick V of the Palatinate who had been newly crowned King of Bohemia. The conflict escalated. Armies and allies were drawn largely along confessional lines. All Europe got involved. Lutherans killed Roman Catholics and Calvinists, Roman Catholics killed Lutherans and Calvinists, Calvinists killed Lutherans and Roman Catholics. And everybody killed Anabaptists (they don't fight back). For thirty years it went on. People literally thought this was Armageddon. Central Europe was laid waste.

There were many reasons for the Thirty Years War (1618–1648) having to do with containing the Hapsburg family's political power and the decay of the Holy Roman Empire. But for the people on the ground, it was a religious war. People were fighting and dying for their version of the religion of the Prince of Peace. The war ended in 1648 with the Peace of Westphalia, which didn't resolve any doctrinal disputes. It simply sent the parties and their armies back to their corners and told them to stay there.

The religion of the prince was the religion of everyone who lived within his territories. If you didn't like it, you could move. Oh, and the choices for religions were: Roman Catholicism, Lutheranism, or Calvinism. Anabaptists were still out of luck (no princes).

INTENTIONAL COMMUNITY IN MODERN PROTESTANTISM

The end of the war established doctrinal purity in a given region. Everyone had to sign on the dotted line. Yet even within these islands of purity a person could subscribe to all the right doctrine and still live like a heathen, and many did. Doctrinal purity, especially "justification by faith alone apart from works," could certainly be twisted to lawless ends. As Protestants looked around at their reformed churches they realized their pure doctrine did not necessarily produce the kind of community pointed to in the New Testament. Calls for "further reform" of the church, though not its doctrine, began to be heard, and small communities of lay people, meeting to encourage one another "in love and good works," began to appear.

Early examples emerged along the Rhine River. The Rhine formed a sort of boundary between Roman Catholic France and Lutheran Germany. It began in Calvinist Switzerland and ended in the Calvinist Netherlands, with several centers of Reformed Christianity along the way. The Rhine also functioned as the major trade route from the Alps to the North Sea, which brought together people of every conceivable "orthodoxy." Roman Catholics, Anabaptists, Calvinists, and Lutherans had to mix. In this environment a type of Christianity developed that focused less on doctrine, and more on the life of the believer—the fruits of faith in individual and communal life.

Defining this movement is a challenge due to its complexity and diversity. It was not a confession, but a way of understanding what it means to be Christian that crossed confessional lines. Known by its Lutheran version as "Pietism," it is a collection of theological emphases—much in the way a disease is a collection of symptoms. Some defining marks of this movement were:

- A concern for further reformation of the church, worked out in the lives of believers in community.

- A strong emphasis on holy living. A Christian is not simply declared righteous, but is actually made righteous by the power of the Holy Spirit.

- The expectation of a quasi-mystical experience of the love of God in justification and the new birth.

- Hope for the world and the expectation that the Holy Spirit will work in the lives of individual believers and in the world through works of mercy, mission, and social reform.

- The use of small groups for cultivating the Christian life.[7]

This way of understanding Christianity was transmitted, not through theological systems and confessions, but through books on practical piety, human contact, and ultimately some perceived contact with God. It avoided squabbles over theological "opinions," which enabled it to move and multiply across confessional and political borders.

One center for this new type of intentional community was the Netherlands. In Leiden, at least since 1629, small groups were meeting for teaching and counsel outside of services. At the university in Utrecht, a professor, Gisbert Voetius (1589–1676) organized his students into small groups for the "precise" observance of the moral law, summarized as loving God and neighbor. This movement came to be known as Precisianism. Jadicus van Lodensteyn (1620–1677), who had been one of Voetius' theology students at Utrecht, later studied under a less dogmatic professor named Johannes Cocceius (1603–1669). In the small groups van Lodentsteyn organized, he brought together Voetius' zeal for holy living and Cocceius' moderate German Calvinism. The focus was practical Christianity, the cultivation of Christian affections, and following the moral law. Disputes over doctrinal issues were forbidden.[8]

Such experiments in Christian community spread. Theodor Unterreyck (1635–1693) of Duisberg also studied in Utrecht and Leiden, and carried the practice of organizing small communities of intentional Christians into the German Reformed Church. In 1665, Unterreyck began these house groups/conventicles in Mühlheim an der Ruhr. Over eight

---

7. Gerdes, "Theological Tenets of Pietism," 25. See also Brown, *Understanding Pietism.*

8. Campbell, *Religion of the Heart,* 73.

years he made these groups an established facet of church life. In 1668 Unterreyck moved to Kassel and spread the small groups there.[9]

They were not limited to Calvinist communities. They jumped to Lutheran and even High-Church Anglican traditions. In 1675 Phillip Jacob Spener (1635–1705) published *Pia Desideria* ("Pious Wishes") which advocated small groups within the German Lutheran church.[10] It is from this work that the term "Pietism" came to be applied to his and similar movements. Spener called the groups he organized *Collegia Pietatis*, colleges of piety. The book served as a manifesto around which Lutheran pastors and laity were drawn into small groups for spiritual encouragement, becoming a powerful force for spiritual renewal, mission, and service to the world. Spener's influence helped a number of Pietists (most importantly August Hermann Franke) get faculty positions at the new University of Halle. Halle became the center of Piestist work, which included care for orphans, schools, and Protestant foreign missions.

Spener's godson became a major experimenter in intentional community. Count Ludwig von Zinzendorf (1700–1760) was a pious noble who invited a group of protestant refugees to live on his estate. Strife among this community caused him to leave his post at court and take an active role in the community. He organized them into smaller companies called "bands" that practiced mutual confession. One night during a religious service, the entire community including Zinzendorf experienced what they understood as a visitation by the Holy Spirit. After this proto-Pentecostal moment, these religious refugees solidified into a movement known as Moravianism with small intentional communities at its core. They didn't at first understand themselves as a new church, but rather a pan-confessional movement.[11]

In England, Anthony Horneck, (1641–1697) is key for Pietism's transfer into Sacramental Anglicanism. Raised in the German Reformed church, Horneck immigrated to England right after the English Civil War. He became a committed Anglican, both in terms of his love for the early

9. Goeters, "Der reformierte Pietismus in Deutschland," 244–46.

10. *Pia Desideria* was originally written as a preface for a new printing of Johann Arndt's *True Christianity* (published in 1606) which claimed that theological orthodoxy is insufficient to produce a truly Christian life.

11. Podmore, *Moravian Church in England*, 6–10. See also Weinlick, *Count Zinzendorf*, 77–79.

church and his sacramental piety. In 1678, he began organizing what were called Religious Societies among groups of young people who had been awakened through his preaching to a need for a deeper spiritual life. The rules that Horneck drew up for the societies included a desire to pursue holiness, charitable work, and avoiding talk of controverted issues of doctrine or church government (which had been at the center of England's civil war). Out of these groups emerged other philanthropic organizations such as the Society for Promoting Christian Knowledge (SPCK), which set about establishing charity schools that were supported by the members the religious societies. The SPCK promoted the establishment of religious societies (and thus charity schools) in every parish in England.[12]

THE WESLEYAN REVIVAL

When we think of the Wesleyan revival we don't usually think of monastic community. We think of preachers roaming the countryside proclaiming the doctrine of the new birth. However, the Wesleyan revival owed its depth and longevity to intentional semi-monastic community adapted from both the Anglican religious societies and the Moravians. Methodism was a pastiche of the experiments in intentional Christian community that had proliferated throughout Protestantism on the Continent and Britain for half a century.

Charles Wesley, as an undergraduate, decided to gather a group of young men to observe the "method of study" prescribed by Oxford University. This method (from which the term "Methodist" derives) dated back to the university's monastic origins, and involved study of the Scriptures and theology on certain days of the week and weekly attendance at the Eucharist. Charles was already familiar with this form of community building. His father, Samuel Wesley, with the encouragement of the SPCK, had established religious societies in his parish in Epworth, modeled on those formed by Horneck. One innovation of the elder Wesley was limiting the number of members to twelve, a practice his son John would later adopt for the intentional Christian communities that sustained the revival.

12. Kisker, *Foundation for Revival.*

John was away from the University in Epworth when his brother began his Oxford "holy club." When he returned to take a position as a Fellow of Lincoln College with responsibility for tutoring undergraduates, he joined them and became a leader. Over time these groups expanded and began to minister with vulnerable populations, visiting prisons and caring for the poor. Their work attracted the attention of Lutheran Pietists in Halle, Germany who recognized Oxford Methodism as a sibling movement.[13]

When John and Charles went to the colonies as missionaries under the auspices of the SPCK they encountered a religious society formed on Horneck's model by a previous SPCK missionary. John nurtured the one in Savannah and established another one in Frederika under lay leadership (an innovation that would become a mark of Methodist intentional community). As missionaries to America, the Wesley brothers also encountered Moravians and their "bands."

The first proto-Methodist Society in London, which met in Fetter Lane, was an amalgam of an Anglican religious society and Moravianism, with its members divided into bands. In a band, four to six society members met with others in similar life circumstances, married women together, single women together, married men together, single men together, to "confess their sins one to another that they may be healed" (James 5:16). In this way, the monastic discipline of confession was adapted for the priesthood of believers. Five questions would be asked at each meeting: What known sins have you committed since our last meeting? What temptations have you met with? How were you delivered? What have you thought, said, or done, of which you doubt whether it be sin or not? Have you nothing you desire to keep secret? Through these questions people were simultaneously led into greater humility and community.

It was the class meeting, however, that became constitutive for Methodist societies. Its origins were pragmatic (the financing of the first Methodist meeting house), but soon the spiritual benefits were obvious. "Many now happily experienced that Christian fellowship of which they had not so much as an idea before. They began to 'bear one another's burdens,' and 'naturally' to 'care for each other.'"[14] Like his father, Wesley

13. Ward, *Protestant Evangelical Awakening*, 4.
14. Wesley, "Plain Account," 262.

limited the number of participants in each class to twelve people. Each week the group would gather to testify, encourage, and hold one another accountable. The question asked of each member each week was: "how does your soul prosper?" To translate into twenty-first century English: "How is your life with God?"

When the discipline of the Methodist Societies was formalized in 1744, both bands and classes were included. The Rule of life for Methodists was simple, taken from Isa 1:16–17. "Cease to do evil, learn to do good." More specifically, those who joined were expected to "continue to evidence their desire of salvation. First, by doing no harm, by avoiding evil in every kind—especially that which is most generally practiced . . . Secondly, by doing good . . . Thirdly, by attending upon all the ordinances of God."[15] This class meeting was the entry point for the society. Anyone who wanted to pursue a more disciplined life with God could join "on trial," a sort of novitiate during which one tried on this rule of life within the community.

These small groups were so important to the revival that John committed to never preach where he could not immediately enfold someone who responded into a class. "I am more and more convinced," he wrote early in his ministry, "that the devil himself desires nothing more than this, that the people of any place should be half-awakened, and then left to themselves to fall asleep again. Therefore I determine, by the grace of God, not to strike one stroke in any place where I cannot follow the blow."[16] The classes and bands were the instruments through which God worked to turn sinners into saints, and by which a communal witness to God's intention for humanity (God's will and kingdom) was manifested.

Like the communities we looked at in the previous chapter, the vast majority of the *de facto* abbots and abbesses, confessors, even the itinerant preachers of this movement were lay people. There were a few clergy involved in Wesleyan Methodism, including John Wesley himself, his brother Charles, John Fletcher, and Thomas Coke, but they were only a handful for all the societies around England. Lay people led the class and band meetings, cared for the poor and the sick and the children, and preached up and down the circuits. Methodism was a lay monastic

15. Wesley, "Nature Design and General Rules," 71–73.
16. Wesley, Journal entry from March 13, 1743, 318.

and preaching order within the larger church. And the larger church was revived.

METHODISM: THE NEXT GENERATION

Very early on, Methodism in America faced a conflict between growth and discipline, between its peculiar monastic organization and the expectations of American denominationalism. By degrees the discipline was relaxed, especially with regard to slavery. The racism of the larger society crept into Methodist societies. Groups began to split off, including the African Methodist Episcopal Church and the African Methodist Episcopal Church, Zion. This tension between building a church or building the Church increased up to the Civil War. By the 1840s, Methodism began to take from other denominations the trappings of "church life" inherited from the European State Church tradition.

In the early nineteenth century Francis Asbury, America's most prominent Methodist bishop, had seen America as a continent, a mission field. The 1865 centenary objective read "Consider the responsibility of Methodists to do their share in educating the conscience of the nation so as to make this a truly Christian Nation."[17] By 1865 the mission of the Methodists was a Christianized nation-state, just like in Europe. This change did not happen overnight, but from the 1830s one could see it happening as the discipline of the semi-monastic preaching order gave way to a Christianity that was very broad, but not very deep, losing both its ability to disciple and form community. Gradually the mainstream of the Methodist Episcopal Church began to see itself as part of the American religious establishment.

Many things led to the abandonment of the practices that formed Methodists. Mutual confession in band meetings was never as widely used in America as in England, especially in the frontier. However, they were common in the more urban areas of the east coast. But by the middle of the nineteenth century in America the bands had virtually disappeared as discipline within the Methodist movement began to wane. The article on bands was omitted from the Discipline of the Methodist Episcopal Church, South in 1854, and of the Methodist Episcopal Church in 1856.

17. Richey, *Early American Methodism*, 39.

The end of Methodism's itinerant preaching order began in 1838. That year, in New York City, one minister was appointed to one church for the first time.[18] This practice then occurred throughout the denomination with single appointments occurring in the larger stations. Placing the "itinerant" within the congregation also changed their role. The itinerant preacher had been primarily an evangelist or apostle—performing the sacraments, preaching and enforcing discipline. Now the clergy were not fully members of the community, and in some sense an imposition into the local culture, yet they no longer had the distance from the community to truly enforce discipline.

The presence of clergy also contributed to the end of the class meeting, the fundamental structure of Methodist intentional community. After settled clergy became common, the worship service, which was becoming more professional and formal, and which featured the minister, began to overshadow the class meeting as the center of community. With a stationed cleric, a member of the society could go directly to him (they were always male) without going first to their class leader (who could be male or female). By mid-nineteenth century class attendance in many churches was less regular or generally practiced than the discipline required, thought it continued, at least on paper, until 1939. That year, when segregation became formalized in the structure of the church, the merged northern and southern branches of Methodism officially dropped the class meeting as defining membership in the society.

Methodism no longer had intentional Christian community at its core. Nonetheless the impulse has remained. There were numerous experiments by Methodists that shaped and preserved this element of Christian renewal. Lucy Rider Meyer (1849–1922) adapted the European deaconess movement to the American Methodist context. In 1885 she founded the Chicago Training School where young women could be equipped to serve the sick and poor in America's urban centers. These women then lived together in voluntary poverty as they ministered. Other associations and programs, such as covenant discipleship groups and Disciple Bible Study, have created Christian community on a small scale. However there has not been within Methodism a broad attempt to renew the larger church through lay intentional community.

18. Hardt, *Soul of Methodism*.

Conclusion

The traditional definition of the church going back to the Reformation has two parts. It is a visible faithful company centered on the Word of God and the Sacraments. That is in fact what Elaine and I mean by monasticism—a visible company of the people of God seeking to be faithful. This does not look simply one way. But these experiments in Christian community are where life in the Spirit is facilitated.

The pattern of renewal occurs over and over in the history of the church. Worldliness creeps into the structures of the church, and God inspires His people to experiment with models of faithfulness. Renewal does not happen when the laity "take control" of the church, but rather when the laity realize we are the church. When we realize *we* are the "Company of the Faithful." It is our charge to center our lives on Jesus—present in Word and Sacrament. "The church is called holy," wrote John Wesley, "because it is holy."[19] This need not be a cloistered holiness, but it is intentional and communal—a holiness in the midst of the stresses and strains of everyday life. If we can recover that, we will recover a church that is vital and effective in the twenty-first century.

19. Wesley, "Of the Church."

FOUR

What the New Methodists Want

It was an unseasonably hot May afternoon and I stood in the shade of a huge tree, thankful for a chance to rest. Along with about fifteen young adults from around the U.S. and Europe, I had just helped to till and plant a community garden in a depressed urban neighborhood. We did the work the old fashioned way, with shovels and rakes. No roto-tillers for us! My task was to move the peeled off strips of sod over to the edge of the lot where they would eventually compost. The wheelbarrow looked like the neighborhood: rickety, cracked, and worn, but it did the job. We finished with surprising speed, bringing to mind the old saying, "Many hands make light the work." Munching on apples, we looked at the soil with satisfaction. In a few weeks rows of vegetables would push up through the earth, announcing the good news. There would be food for hungry neighbors.

SCHOOLS FOR CONVERSION

We were participants in a School for Conversion, an alternative form of theological education that teaches Christians how to live in new monastic communities. As my gaze moved from the new garden to abandoned storefronts and shabby houses I thought about all that we had learned thus far in the school. We were a motley crew from many denominations, our common desire being to live the gospel in small, missional communities. I was twice as old as my companions, a fact that elicited praise from one young man. He said it is rare for someone of my generation, especially a theologian, to take an interest in the new monasticism. He also said the movement needs the stability of Christians who've lived the faith for a long time. Of course he said these things respectfully, but no matter how he framed his words, it was a hard truth to hear. Folk my age, I am sorry to say, are generally protectors of the status quo, or as Dorothy Day put it, the "filthy rotten system."[1] My generation seems to be more focused on paying for long term care insurance than the transformation of the world. It's embarrassing to see how much we are not like our founder John Wesley, who hoped to die poor and asked that his last bit of money be given to those who dug his grave.

Our teacher was Jonathan Wilson-Hartgrove, a leading voice of the new monasticism, having authored several books on the topic and helping to found the Schools for Conversion.[2] He would likely make a self-deprecating joke about talking too much if he heard me say he's a leading voice, but the truth is, Jonathan is a leader of extraordinary depth, maturity and wisdom, one whose life incarnates what he teaches. Jonathan's sense of humor is one of the gifts that help him to open the imagination of the rest of us.

The schools meet several times a year on site at new monastic communities around the United States and in South America. There are several courses to choose from, including one on following a rule of life and contemplative practices. About thirty people gather from diverse backgrounds to spend a few days in classes, conversation, hands-on ministry, and joining the rhythms of the community in praying a daily office. The communities differ widely from one another. Some are urban, some rural, some have been around for a long time, and some are just a few years old. Their forms of daily prayer or rule of life also vary. Jonathan and Leah Wilson-Hartgrove established Rutba House in 2003 in Walltown, an old neighborhood in Durham, North Carolina.

1. Dorothy Day was the founder of the Catholic Worker Movement in the early 20th century. Day is one of the patron saints of the new monasticism. Her autobiography is *The Long Loneliness*. For more information on Day and the Catholic Worker Movement, see http://www.catholicworker.com/.

2. Jonathan tells the story of his trip to Baghdad with a peacemaking team at the outset of the war in Iraq, and how the experiences there led him and Leah to name their house Rutba, in *To Baghdad and Beyond*. The text used for the Schools for Conversion 101 is edited by The Rutba House, *Schools for Conversion*. Jonathan's most recent books which have helped immensely in my research on the new monasticism are *Free to Be Bound* and *New Monasticism*.

So here I was in Springfield, Massachusetts leaning on a shovel with Norwegian divinity students, wondering how many days it would take the carrots to pop through. We were full of questions. New monastic communities, we learned, are made up of Christians choosing to live in intentional community. The new "monks" are ordinary people like us, single and married, some with families. The people have ordinary jobs as teachers, social workers and grocery store clerks. Okay, I said "like us," but there don't seem to be many "professional" theologians among them. Which says much more about the spiritual condition of us theologians, I'm afraid, than a lack of theology in the communities.

EVANGELISM THROUGH THE NEW MONASTICISM

Rather than being cloistered away *from* the world, the new monks form communities to be salt and light *for* the world. In this way they are kenotic, emptying themselves for the sake of their neighbors. Most of them choose downward mobility as a way of life. Yes, very counter cultural. Not at all the American Dream. Which is why this will not become the next big church growth scheme.

The word "evangelism" scarcely came up in the School for Conversion, but everything about the new monasticism is evangelistic. That is, if you understand evangelism holistically.[3] The communities aim to provide an alternative vision to how life can be. That phrase from the Lord's Prayer, "thy will be done on earth as it is in heaven" is kind of a vision statement for the new monks, who long to live in such a way that the earth gets a delicious taste of heaven because of the community. The new monks believe in the manner of Lesslie Newbigin that "it is surely a fact of inexhaustible significance that what our Lord left behind Him was not a book,

---

3. In my classes on evangelism at the beginning of the semester, I give students my definition of evangelism, which is what shapes the content of our class: Evangelism is the holistic initiation of persons into the holy life revealed in Jesus Christ, anchored in the church, empowered by the Holy Spirit, yielded to the reign of God, for the transformation of the world. It's a bit creedal when you think about it, and a bit long. But with this definition put into practice, we could indeed bring renewal to the church and a whole lot of goodness to the world. For more about my understanding of holistic evangelism in postmodern culture, see Heath, *Mystic Way of Evangelism*. For a wonderful book on the exemplary holistic evangelism practiced by women in the nineteenth century, see Laceye Warner, *Saving Women*.

nor a creed, nor a system of thought, nor a rule of life, but a visible community. He committed the entire work of salvation to that community."[4] They would differ somewhat with Newbigin over the rule of life, as a good rule helps everyone stay right side up. And lots of new monks are creedal, read plenty and think deeply. But Newbigin's emphasis on the primacy of community is a hallmark of the new monasticism.

It all made me think of John Wesley, how he insisted that members of Methodist societies follow a rule of life as a community.[5] The early Methodists worked mostly among the poor and marginalized, "spreading scriptural holiness through the land." Their evangelistic method was a combination of social justice and spiritual formation carried out in community. While people often first encountered Methodism through a preaching service, they were evangelized in the class and band meetings, in relationships with members of the community. The Methodist societies, class, and band meetings were not exactly a monastic order. Yet much of what they practiced had parallels in monastic life.

Early Methodism was a holiness movement that evangelized people both inside and outside the church. To frame it with my definition of evangelism, Methodism was a holiness movement that *initiated people into a holy life, revealed in Jesus Christ, anchored in the church, empowered by the Holy Spirit, surrendered to the reign of God, for the transformation of the world*. What we have in the new monasticism is in fact a holiness movement, one that is larger than any denomination but that resonates deeply with the Methodist soul.

The New Methodists

Ironically, in a day in which Methodist church membership is in a nosedive, growing numbers of young Methodists are feeling called to rigorous faith, to holiness of heart and life. This is despite the meaninglessness of membership vows in a majority of Methodist churches.[6] Often shunning

4. Newbigin, *Household of God*, 20.

5. The General Rules of the United Societies (later called the General Rules of the Methodist Church) were first published in 1743. A slightly revised version can still be found in the United Methodist *Book of Discipline*, but most Methodists neither know of their existence nor practice a Methodist rule of life.

6. Out of a desire to be "inclusive" and "non-threatening" many United Methodist

the traditional ordination track, the new Methodists nonetheless come to seminary to learn how to serve Jesus.[7] They are jaded toward institutional politics, unwilling to surrender their spiritual passion to what they see as an ordination system that weeds out pioneers and rewards bureaucrats. They are risk-takers, innovators, a new breed of old fashioned Methodists. To go back to what I said in chapter one, they recognize the club for what it is.

Like Dietrich Bonhoeffer who coined the term "new monasticism,"[8] they believe that the church of the twenty-first century needs to be a new kind of church. It must be marked by a radical commitment to live the Sermon on the Mount. And with Russian Orthodox martyr Mother Maria Skobtsova, they believe that it needs to be earthy, "a monasticism for the world."[9] Emerging from their courses in Methodist history and doctrine, these students look around and ask, "What happened?" They come to my office asking how they can remain in the United Methodist Church and still answer their call, because what they long to do is other. It is emergent.[10] It is hard for them to imagine Jesus (or Wesley) doing most of the things that we do to grow the Methodist church. They are appalled by the conventional church growth wisdom that "at the end of the day what

Churches invite people to join the church with no preparation of any kind. It reminds me of the old *Let's Make a Deal* television game show, with people invited at the end of worship to "come on down" to unite themselves to the mystery hidden behind the doors. Will it be a goat or a new car? Will membership mean being in a club or having to tithe?

7. The new Methodists as I am using the term, does not refer to a breakaway group of Methodists called The New Methodist Conference. It refers to people within the United Methodist Church who are drawn toward new monasticism.

8. Quoted widely in new monastic resources including the Northumbria Community website, Bonhoeffer makes the statement in a letter written to his brother, Karl Friedrick on January 14, 1935. Bonhoeffer, *Testament to Freedom*, 424.

9. Forest, "Introduction," 23.

10. While some of them want to form and lead emergent churches, many feel called to the new monasticism, one form of the emergent phenomenon. I believe that the best of the emerging church is deeply significant in the way that Pentecostalism has been, ushering in a new emphasis on missional presence in the world. My hunch is that over the long haul the new monasticism will have the kind of lasting impact on the church and the world that has always been true for monasticism. Think of the Benedictines, for example. For more on the phenomenon and characteristics of emerging churches and a broad array of examples in the U.S. and the U.K., see Gibbs and Bolger, *Emerging Churches* and Jones, *New Christians*. The leading spokesperson in the emerging church is Brian McLaren, author of numerous books including *Generous Orthodoxy*.

counts is butts in pews."[11] What they want is butts out of pews, into the neighborhood, transforming the world. Especially among the poor.

The new Methodists are longing for Spring, for a rebirth of the best of our tradition. What the new Methodists want is to go the way of early Methodism only retooled for postmodern times. But can they do this and remain in the UMC? Can they do this and still be ordained? The answers to these questions rest partly in the *Book of Discipline*, and partly in the willingness of boards of ordained ministry and bishops to cooperate with this move of the Holy Spirit. It rests in institutional willingness to rethink and retool the itinerant system. Perhaps most importantly, it rests in the tenacity of the new Methodists to move into new life forms without leaving the mother ship, even if they are denied ordination in the process.

Because really, let's be honest, the Lord Jesus Christ would not get ordained in the United Methodist Church if he were to come and carry out his earthly work today. For one thing he couldn't get through the process in the three years of ministry before his crucifixion. And even if he could, his insistence on being the Light of the World would be seen as exclusive by some boards of ordained ministry, and his friendships with women would scandalize others. The bishop would not like his homelessness. His poverty would make a Master of Divinity degree impossible. You see what I mean. This business of following Jesus is going to sometimes mean that foxes have holes and birds have nests but we have nowhere to lay our head in the ordination process. My suspicion is that if enough new Methodists are stubborn about staying in the church but radical about following Jesus, with or without ordination, with or without financial remuneration for their ministry, they will bring about systemic change.

But you need to know that the new Methodists aren't the only ones asking some hard questions. Methodist historian and Dean of Perkins School of Theology, William Lawrence ponders, "Does it really matter if The United Methodist Church endures? Or is the far more vital issue the mission of the church?"[12] For Methodism to recover health, he says, it will need to recover its missional identity, something that has been swallowed up in church marketing, randomly launched programs and projects, and an institutional process of "lurching across a sea of ideas in the hope of

---

11. A phrase learned by several of my students in a training event they attended.

12. Lawrence, *Methodism in Recovery*, 21.

latching onto something that will actually work."[13] I'm not so sure we are even lurching across the sea. I'd say we are in the doldrums, waiting for ideas to drift by so we can snag them.

What we need, instead, is right in front of us in our churches and seminary classrooms: missional Christians who are willing to risk everything for the sake of the gospel. We need the new Methodists. We need to encourage rather than thwart the new generation of John Wesleys and Phoebe Palmers among us, and help them develop and lead new monastic communities so they can help us remember why we are here. With the Schools for Conversion and other resources, so much has already been done to help Methodists find our way back home to our vocation.

TWELVE MARKS

So what does a new monastic community really look like? There are twelve "marks" that are common to these groups, regardless of their theological bent or geographic location. The marks were defined in June, 2004 when Jonathan Wilson-Hartgrove and a number of other leaders of new monastic communities gathered for a conference in order to "discern a possible shape of a new monasticism."[14] As Jonathan comments, "Some marks are more visible in some communities than others, yet all recognize the work of the Holy Spirit in their common forms of life sketched in the twelve marks. The list is not to be understood as the necessary shape of all faithful witness. Rather, it helps name the unique witness these neo-monastic communities have to offer the rest of the church."[15] To map out a plan for new monasticism as United Methodists, a good place to start is a consideration of the twelve marks in light of the Methodist history, theology and practice already discussed in chapter three. Do the marks, in other words, reflect Methodist sensibilities? Are they compatible with the best of Methodist theology and praxis? Let's take a look:

13. Ibid., 81.
14. Rutba House, *Schools for Conversion*, x.
15. Ibid.

1. Relocation to the abandoned places of Empire.

2. Sharing economic resources with fellow community members and the needy among us.

3. Hospitality to the stranger.

4. Lament for racial divisions within the church and our communities combined with the active pursuit of a just reconciliation.

5. Humble submission to Christ's body, the church.

6. Intentional formation in the way of Christ and the rule of the community along the lines of the old novitiate.

7. Nurturing common life among members of intentional community.

8. Support for celibate singles alongside monogamous married couples and their children.

9. Geographical proximity to community members who share a common rule of life.

10. Care for the plot of God's earth given to us along with support of our local economies.

11. Peacemaking in the midst of violence and conflict resolution within communities along the lines of Matthew 18.

12. Commitment to a disciplined contemplative life.[16]

You don't have to read a lot of John Wesley or the *Book of Discipline* to recognize many familiar themes. Every one of these is consistent with solid, Wesleyan theology. We sing these themes from our hymnal every week. What is especially consistent with historic Methodism is the seamless blend of social holiness and evangelical piety.

A FEW EXAMPLES

In general new monastic communities are small, and the ways in which they share a common life vary greatly. In some cases members live communally in a big house or a network of several houses in the same neigh-

16. Ibid., xii–xiii. Also, see www.newmonasticism.org for short articles and helpful links.

borhood. Church of the Servant King in Eugene, Oregon, is a model where most of the members live in the same neighborhood in the city. Some new monastic communities consider themselves to be a congregation and hold worship on Sundays in their houses or, like Rutba House, attend the same church in their neighborhood. Others follow a rule of life and perhaps pray a daily office together, but the members go to different churches on Sundays. Nehemiah House and its community, for example, attend several different churches. Many if not most communities are founded in poor neighborhoods that have been "abandoned by Empire," in order to live the gospel there. The Simple Way, founded by Shane Claiborne and others and described in *Irresistible Revolution,* is a well-known example of this kind of community. Renaissance House in Richmond, Indiana is another, formed for men who are mentally ill and often homeless.[17] The amount of property, money and material goods that are held in common varies among the communities. For the most part they function a bit like an extended family or a small village, with family-like relationships, sharing, and the inevitable conflicts that arise in families. Indeed, it is the friction and struggle of life in community that makes it difficult, and the inability to work through conflict in healthy ways is the primary reason communities, like "ordinary" congregations, fall apart. Yet there is no substitute for genuine community in healing wounds and cultivating holiness. Community really is a "school for conversion," leading us into the freedom and loving interconnectedness for which we were created.

I have briefly described several primary models of new monastic communities, but there are many variations.[18] The Internet has made possible additional networking opportunities for like-minded communities such as the Northumbria Community, which includes a mother house in the U.K. (Nether Springs), and satellite communities around the U.K. and in the U.S. Anyone who wants to can access the website for Northumbria Community in order to pray the daily office and use other resources provided, thus have a bit of a link to their community. While the web is an important tool for some aspects of the new monasticism, as members of every community with which I have had contact emphasize, the heart

17. For a wonderful introduction to new monasticism and the poor written from an evangelical perspective, see Bessenecker, *New Friars.*

18. For an extended discussion of the kinds of communities and their practices, see Wilson-Hartgrove, *New Monasticism,* as well as *Schools for Conversion.*

of new monasticism is relationships: actual flesh and blood community where people know one another, share life, and reach out together to their neighbors. It is telling that many new monastic communities do not even have websites.

Are new monastic communities with their twelve marks a possibility for United Methodists today? According to the 2004 *Book of Discipline*, the answer, or at least the beginning of an answer, is yes. Paragraph 161.b of The Social Principles states: "We further recognize the movement to find new patterns of Christian nurturing communities such as Koinonia Farms, certain monastic and other religious orders, and some types of corporate church life. We urge the church to seek ways of understanding the needs and concerns of such Christian groups and to find ways of ministering to them and through them."[19] The part that is unanswered is what it means for the UMC to "minister to them and through them." And it's telling that the one example of a new monastic community that is given in Paragraph 161.b is Koinonia Farms, an amazing agricultural community founded in 1942 by Clarence Jordan. Koinonia Farms is the birthplace of Habitat for Humanity, a ministry to which many Methodists give time, energy, and financial support. Koinonia Farms modeled racial reconciliation from the outset, a courageous stance that brought persecution. But neither Clarence nor Koinonia Farms are Methodist.

It's high time we changed that, don't you think? Not that we change Clarence or Koinonia Farms, they are wonderful,[20] but wouldn't it be great for the 2012 *Book of Discipline* to give some examples of Methodist new monastic communities? And wouldn't it be even better if it contained sections that detail how the appointment system works for elders who are called to bi-vocational ministry in new monastic communities, and how deacons and lay people fit into the plan? These are all matters that have to be addressed because being called to lead a new monastic community as a clergy person is a bit like being the eunuch Jesus describes in Matthew 19:12. There is a voluntary poverty that goes with this call, a kenotic emptying of much that is considered "normal" compensation for a clergy life. Not everyone is called to the new monasticism, and not just any Elder

19. *Book of Discipline of the United Methodist Church 2004.* Interestingly, this paragraph was removed from the 2008 *Book of Discipline*.

20. For a fine introduction to the history and practices of the Koinonia Farm see their website, "Koinonia," at http://www.koinoniapartners.org/whatis.html.

or Deacon is right for this kind of mission. The guidelines for this kind of community in the United Methodist tradition cannot be exactly the same as for just any congregation. There are other issues, too, that must be addressed.

We will need to distinguish between new monastic communities that are also congregations, and those that are anchored in more established congregations. How is a new monastic new church start different from other kinds of new church starts? What kind of training or "boot camp" would the new leaders require? The possibility of monastic orders for Methodists also comes to mind. What would an Order look like? What would the novitiate consist of, and how would leaders be prepared? The degree of intentional community is also a matter requiring discernment. These are a few of the issues that will need attention if the United Methodist Church takes seriously the holiness movement that is afoot today.

In the next chapter we will begin to imagine how Methodism can and should systematically and wholeheartedly advance the new monasticism as a vital form of holistic evangelism in the twenty-first century.

FIVE

Spring

I am more concerned about the vitality of the one, holy, catholic, apostolic church than about the survival of the United Methodist Church. I suspect John Wesley would say the same thing. At the same time, while I am skeptical about the future of denominationalism, I love Wesleyan theology and am proud of much in the Methodist tradition. I want the best of Methodist theology and practice to survive. That is why I am convinced that the United Methodist Church can and should pioneer new monastic ministries. The new monasticism is a new holiness movement, and what could be more Wesleyan than that? Methodist monasticism should take at least three forms: an apostolic, contemplative monastic order both for clergy and laity, new monastic new church starts, and the development of new monastic communities that are anchored in existing congregations. Equipping people, both clergy and laity, to serve in these ministries will require some new models of theological education and a much greater emphasis on new church starts among the poor. While I agree with Scott that monasticism is essentially a lay movement, in Methodism we can and should create ways for clergy who are called to the new monasticism to answer that call as United Methodists.

THE NEED FOR A RULE OF LIFE

Regardless of the form of new monasticism, a rule of life will be essential. Marjorie Thompson reminds us that a good rule of life is a supportive structure that helps us have the freedom, light and space that we require in order to grow into shalom.[1] A rule of life reminds me of some window washers I saw recently while waiting for a train in downtown Dallas. There were four of them suspended on ropes attached to the roof of a skyscraper. Down they came, dancing like fastidious spiders with their buckets and squeegees. The ropes gave them the ability to do what otherwise would have been impossible, descending the sheer face of the building in order to serve its inhabitants. Each worker had a suction device on a handle, which he used to stabilize himself while he washed the windows. Slowly they came, until each one landed safely on the sidewalk and the windows sparkled in the sun. Their ropes and stabilizers were a kind of "rule" to guide, protect, and give them freedom to accomplish their mission.

Without a rule, or disciplined practices, our spiritual lives easily become disordered. The Rule of St. Benedict is probably the best-known monastic rule of life, dating back some 1,500 years, and is exemplary in its moderation and "livability" for ordinary Christians. Joan Chittister's *Wisdom Distilled from the Daily* provides a good introduction to the rule for lay people.[2] And, as Scott pointed out earlier, the rule was created by a layperson for lay people!

The Rule of St. Benedict has three components: conversion, obedience, and stability. Jon Stock, Tim Otto, and Jonathan Wilson-Hartgrove have written a critical analysis of the Benedictine rule from an evangelical perspective, demonstrating that the rule is grounded deeply in the Bible and is intended to cultivate holiness of heart and life.[3] (People from evangelical backgrounds especially appreciate this kind of book, reassuring them of the biblical grounding of an unfamiliar "Catholic" spiritual practice.) With some modification the Benedictine rule can be embraced by people from any Christian tradition, although the rule of stability (staying put in one place permanently, with the same group of Christians) is nearly impossible for United Methodist clergy, who take vows to itinerate. I suppose you could say that in this matter we take vows of *in*stability.

---

1. Thompson, *Soul Feast*, 145.

2. Joan Chittister is a Benedictine sister who has authored more than forty books and is an extraordinary, ecumenical voice for women's rights and other justice and spirituality issues. The original Rule of Benedict is also found online in multiple sources, including the website for the Order of St. Benedict, http://www.osb.org/rb/.

3. Stock et al., *Inhabiting the Church*.

The most obvious place for Methodists to begin thinking about a rule is with a reading of Wesley's General Rules for Methodist Societies.[4] These are organized into three categories (my paraphrase):

1. First, do no harm.

2. Do all the good you can.

3. Practice individual and corporate spiritual disciplines.

As did St. Benedict with his three-fold rule, underneath each precept Wesley detailed a variety of applications, such as refusing to own slaves and practicing frugality. While we may not want to incorporate the applications of the three rules exactly as Wesley wrote them, we can learn much from them and incorporate their spirit. It is striking to see how many of Wesley's applications are consistent with the twelve marks of the new monasticism. The use of these three rules would be more than adequate for a Methodist new monastic rule today, especially if fleshed out with contemporary practices. Kevin M. Watson's recent volume, *Blueprint for Discipleship* provides a readable and inspiring discussion for lay people and could be used in developing a rule patterned after Wesley's General Rules.

MEMBERSHIP VOWS AND THE RULE OF LIFE

Another alternative that could be helpful to the whole church, would be for the rule to follow the fivefold structure of membership vows in the United Methodist Church.[5] When joining the United Methodist Church, candidates vow "to be loyal to the United Methodist Church and uphold it" with their "prayers, presence, gifts, service, and witness."[6] While each United Methodist new monastic community could adapt details of the fivefold rule somewhat to its mission and location, the use of the five membership vows as a framework could help the rule have a degree of consistency across diverse communities in the tradition. For example, the rule could look like this:

4. The General Rules are found in the *United Methodist Book of Discipline*, ¶103.

5. It could help the whole church if it was included in membership preparation resources, for example, and offered as a model of covenant faithfulness that any disciple could embrace.

6. The word "witness" was added at General Conference, 2008, to help members understand the evangelistic commission of every Christian (*United Methodist Hymnal*, 48).

Prayers
- We will pray daily
- We will use a variety of forms of prayer such as the reflective reading of Scripture and other spiritual texts, confession, the prayer of examen, intercession, journaling, and contemplation
- We will regularly fast

Presence
- We will practice a contemplative stance in order to be present to God, the world, and ourselves
- We will be hospitable to our neighbors in our families, neighborhoods and workplaces
- We will be hospitable to our faith community through participation in our worship, fellowship and mission

Gifts
- We will honor and care for the gift of the earth and its resources, practicing ecologically responsible living, striving for simplicity rather than excessive consumption
- We will practice generosity in sharing our material resources, including money, within and beyond this community
- We will use our spiritual gifts, talents and abilities to serve God within and beyond this community

Service
- We will serve God and neighbor out of gratitude for the love of God
- We will practice mutual accountability with a covenant group within the community, for how we serve God and neighbor
- We will practice regular Sabbath as a means of renewal so that we can lovingly serve God and neighbor

Witness
- We will practice racial and gender reconciliation
- We will resist evil and injustice
- We will pursue peace with justice
- We will share the redeeming, healing, creative love of God in word, deed and presence in order to invite others to Christian discipleship

I commit to this rule of life and to the well-being of this community, out of gratitude to God who forgives, heals, and makes all things new. May my life be a blessing within and beyond God's church, for the transformation of the world.[7]

This kind of a rule could be followed by members of a new monastic congregation, or by members of a new monastic order, whether clergy, lay, or both. This example of a Wesleyan rule could be modified for more intense communal arrangements in terms of economic redistribution, or adapted in other ways for a specific order's vocation.

MONASTIC ORDERS

In the history of the church, orders have been founded by prophetic reformers of the church, people like Saint Benedict, Saint Francis, Saint Ignatius of Loyola, and Mother Teresa of Calcutta. While most Methodists don't think of monastic orders as a Protestant option, as we have seen, early Methodism had much in common with a lay monastic movement. To be a member of a Methodist society entailed much that was similar to being a member of an order. Today we have within Methodism the Order of Elders, and the Order of St. Luke, a society that focuses on liturgical renewal in the church.

PATRON SAINTS FOR METHODIST NEW MONASTICISM

We do not canonize Protestant saints in the manner of the Catholic and Orthodox churches, but we have the equivalent of canonized saints in heroes of faith like John Wesley and a generation later in the American Methodist, Phoebe Palmer. Palmer, the mother of the nineteenth century holiness movement, embodied just about everything that the new monasticism holds dear. The only label she would have used for herself was that she was a "Bible Christian," but Palmer had every quality necessary

---

7. This is the rule of life for New Day, a United Methodist new monastic community in Dallas, TX. http://www.newdaydallas.org. More information about New Day is found in the next chapter.

in the Catholic world to be considered the founder of an order.[8] The di-
minutive Methodist was a lay reformer of the Methodist Church, a revival
preacher, Bible teacher, and lay theologian who led over 25,000 people
to Christ.[9] She was our own Methodist mystic[10] who practiced holistic
evangelism, emphasized holiness of heart and life, and wrote many books
and articles including a landmark text on the right of women to engage
in public ministry. Palmer followed a disciplined rule of life throughout
her life, faithful to her Methodist upbringing. Her Tuesday Meetings for
the Promotion of Holiness generated a following of disciples who went
on to incarnate her spirituality in their social justice activism and spiritual leadership. Bishops and theologians were among Palmer's disciples.
Her life and teaching left a permanent legacy in the Wesleyan holiness
tradition.[11] For all these reasons Palmer is a fine exemplar for a "patron
saint" of a new monastic order of United Methodists. The Order could be
named after Phoebe Palmer, John Wesley, or another saint. It could also
be named for its missional emphasis, such as Mother Teresa's order, The
Missionaries of Charity.

The Order would be contemplative because it would be grounded in
the practices of prayer, a truly Wesleyan and new monastic emphasis. And
it would be apostolic because of its commitment to holistic evangelism as
described in the rule of life.

To become full members of the Order, persons would undergo a
novitiate during which they would learn the theory and practice of new
monasticism especially as articulated in the rule of life. This would be
done through mentoring relationships with existing members, theological education (I'll say more about this presently), and participation in the
Order's community and its mission. After a one-to-three-year novitiate
the candidate could, with the blessing of the local community, become a
full member of the Order. Membership would be understood kenotically,

---

8. For more on the role of religious vocation and what constitutes a call to such in the
Catholic church, see Adams, "Religious Life," 817–22.

9. Tucker and Liefeld, *Daughters of the Church*, 263.

10. By mystic I mean a classical Christian mystic of the same caliber as St. Teresa of
Avila and Saint Catherine of Siena. Palmer's Christian mysticism was distinctly Wesleyan
and oriented toward the Bible.

11. For an extended treatment of the life and thought of Phoebe Palmer see my book,
Naked Faith.

in terms of responsibility and service. Every year members of the Order would be given an opportunity to renew their membership covenant. By having an annual renewal of covenant all members of the Order would be accountable to one another for their membership covenant. This practice would cohere with Wesley's General Rules in that Wesley specified that members should watch over one another in love, in the small communities of classes and bands. An annual renewal of covenant is practiced in a number of new monastic communities, including Church of the Servant King in Eugene, Oregon, where the covenant is called the "Statement of Commitment."[12]

At the end of the General Rules, Wesley writes: "If there be any among us who observe them not, who habitually break any of them, let it be known unto them who watch over that soul as they who must give an account. We will admonish him of the error of his ways. We will bear with him for a season. But then, if he repent not, he hath no more place among us. We have delivered our own souls."[13] The annual renewal of covenant is less harsh than Wesley's expulsion of errant members, but it would do much to preserve the importance and meaning of the covenant vows.

The Order would not be a cloistered community, since it would be apostolic, sent into the world with the good news. A community could either be anchored in an existing congregation, taking part in the worship and mission activities of a local UMC, or it could be a local congregation. In the former case the leader of a community could be an elder, deacon, local pastor, or suitably trained lay leader. For the latter option it would be necessary for the leader of the community to be an elder, local pastor, or possibly a deacon,[14] for the administration of the sacraments.

Navigating the Waters of Appointments

One of the challenges in appointing elders to new monastic ministries will be to navigate the waters of appointment. First there is the issue of

12. Stock, *Inhabiting the Church*, 117.

13. *Book of Discipline*, ¶103.

14. At the 2008 General Conference a new option was made possible for some deacons in some appointments to be permitted to administer the sacraments. The outworking of this new possibility remains to be seen, but it appears to make more feasible the formation of new monastic communities led by non-itinerating deacons.

itineracy. If new monastic communities are treated as extension appointments, then the elder could serve a given community for a much longer time, cultivating the stability that is necessary in monastic communities. If new monastic communities are to thrive it will be essential for their leaders to have the gifts, call, and training needed for a new monastic appointment. Not just anyone can serve as an abbot or abbess, which is the historic name for the spiritual leader of a monastic community. What this means is that bishops and district superintendents will need to support and facilitate the process in three ways. First, they need to know and affirm the mission of monastic communities, and why they are important to the life of the whole church. Second, they need to be careful only to appoint persons to these ministries who have the appropriate training and gifts for monastic life. Third, these appointments need to be long term. This last stipulation is grounded in the reality of what Saint Benedict has taught the church for the last 1,500 years. Communities and their leaders need to practice the rule of stability.

For communities anchored in established congregations, leadership could be provided by deacons, local pastors, or lay leaders rather than itinerating elders. In this case the community could serve as a missional branch of the mother church, a sub-congregation with a specific contemplative, apostolic vocation. The Missionaries of Charity community in Dallas, for example, worships at St. James Catholic Church just down the street, but their ministries of prayer and presence in their impoverished neighborhood are their way of living their missional vocation.

METHODIST BEGUINES

One example of a form of new monasticism that could minister to single mothers and widows is for a church to establish a household for several individuals and/or families. It could be a contemporary form of the old Beguine model of monasticism. In every church I have served as pastor, there have been a number of older widows who lived alone, usually in homes with three or four bedrooms. Most of these widows had trouble taking care of a large house and property, yet they did not want to give up their independence or move out of the home where they raised their families. While they had the asset of a large home, a number of these widows lived on very limited income and some suffered from chronic loneliness. There were also, in these churches, single parents with children. Like the widows, most of the single parents struggled to make ends meet and suffered from loneliness as they worked hard to raise their families without a spouse. Within a new monastic community in an established church, some of these widows and single parent families could share a household, cutting costs for everyone and providing a loving family for all. This kind of arrangement is common in the new monasticism, and can work very well in any context. With the dramatic rise in home foreclosures, unemployment, and other economic challenges that lie ahead, increasing numbers of suburban families are going to need these kinds of options in order to avoid homelessness. The church should be at the forefront with forming intentional community among those who are at risk in these ways.

ANCHOR CHURCHES AND MONASTIC NEW CHURCH STARTS

In addition to forming new monastic communities that are anchored in established congregations, the United Methodist Church should facilitate new church starts that are free-standing new monastic communities. One model that could work very well in suburban, urban, or rural contexts is a house church that would grow through expansion into a network of house churches that meet together monthly or quarterly for a larger worship gathering. Each house church in the community would follow the rule of life and would meet weekly for worship and spiritual formation. In a given neighborhood several households could live in community and form one house church. A lead team of two or more bi-vocational elders or an elder and deacons or local pastors could serve this kind of networked community, equipping the leaders of the house churches. By using houses rather than church buildings, and a team of bi-vocational pastors, this kind of community could be much more flexible and adaptable to the missional needs of local neighborhoods, and could use its economic resources almost entirely in mission rather than to support expensive buildings, salaries and benefit packages.[15]

15. For more on the use of house church networks and their missional strength in the underground church of China and in the early church see Alan Hirsch, *Forgotten Ways*.

A PREFERENCE FOR BI-VOCATIONAL MINISTRY

Bi-vocational ministry has always been part of the Methodist tradition, especially among the poor. Yet bi-vocational ministry has not been a preferred model because of the ways in which it has been abusive of clergy, expecting them to work fulltime for the church and at their jobs. The logistics of a new monastic community would prevent this kind of abuse because new monastic communities are by nature small and participatory, with ministry belonging to the members and not to a professional staff. The growth of this form of church is through the multiplication of small communities rather than the bloating of one congregation. Bi-vocational ministry makes the most sense in this context.

Another important reason to prefer bi-vocational ministry in new monastic contexts, is that it provides a powerful kenotic witness to a world that has come to associate church, particularly evangelism, with greed and the abuse of power. David Kinnaman's devastating new study, *Unchristian*, reveals that over eighty percent of people ages sixteen to twenty-nine in the United States have a negative view of Christianity and the church because of the hypocrisy and self-serving swagger of Christians.[16] These perceptions are grounded in actual experiences of greed and abuse at the hands of exploitive Christians. The only way the church is going to change these perceptions is to return to a kenotic, missional vocation in which our identity is found in Philippians 2.

Another model of new monastic new church start that uses a team of bi-vocational pastors, is for a new monastic community to be appointed to a declining urban setting, using an existing church building that has either been closed or is near closure. Rather than trying to revitalize the church through the usual means, the community would develop as a new monastic community. Again, teams of two to four bi-vocational pastors, using a building that is already owned by the conference, could develop powerful ministries that would not be centered on securing their salaries and benefits and conference apportionments in order to be in ministry among the poor. As it stands now, most new church start initiatives in the United Methodist Church are focused on affluent, new suburban populations, where the goal is to grow the next mega-church. New monastic

---

16. Kinnaman and Lyons, *Unchristian*, 25–27.

church starts show a preference for the forsaken places of empire, which is exactly where Wesley and most of the early Methodists spent their lives.

Theological Education for New Monastic Methodists

Those who will develop and lead United Methodist new monastic communities will need a good theological education with a special dual emphasis on spiritual formation and community development. In order to accommodate these emphases, seminaries could develop certificate programs or concentrations in new monastic studies. Ideally the student would live in a new monastic community where he or she would practice living the rule of life and missional presence in a neighborhood, while completing a seminary education. The development of these programs could be accomplished with creativity and visionary leadership that would include an agreement among United Methodist seminaries to cooperate rather than compete.

The United Methodist Church currently has thirteen seminaries across the United States. Why couldn't a consortium of three or four U.M. seminaries jointly sponsor several new monastic houses in diverse locations, and jointly develop a curriculum around the new monasticism? For example there could be a new monastic community in an urban Latino or African American neighborhood (like Rutba House), one in the rural south (like Koinonia Farms), and one in a working poor community in the Midwest (like Renaissance House). Each of these houses/communities would be hosted by a U.M. seminary. Each house would have a resident elder or deacon who functions as a mentor to the students. Ideally the resident elder would be bi-vocational, modeling the kind of life most new monastic community members will live. After all, it isn't a fulltime job for a deacon or elder to live with several other people in a neighborhood in a ministry of presence. MDiv students could complete one year of their three year program in residence in any one of the new monastic communities, and get credit for their degree in their home school. Students would pay a moderate fee for room and board, which would also go toward the upkeep of the house. Living and working in these communities could also be part of students' internships or field education. Though the student residents of these houses would change as students matriculate and graduate, the resident elder or deacon (and family, if they have one) and perhaps another family would be permanent members of the community.

The consortium model described above, would be a good beginning, but to provide even more in-depth theological preparation the United Methodist Church could convert one of its failing campgrounds (there are many) into a monastery with an educational mission. Students would complete their entire theological education in this institution. Faculty and students would live in community, follow a rule of life together, order the day around a daily office, and integrate academic work with practices of justice and peace throughout their degree programs. By reclaiming an old campground, which is already owned by the denomination, the monastery could easily develop organic gardens, walking trails, and other natural features to help students learn about ecological ethics and creation care. Once again, the Benedictines have a rich history from which Methodists could learn how to create this kind of seminary.

An urban alternative to this plan would be to rehab one of the hulking, beautiful, gothic cathedrals that are virtually empty now, turning it into a monastery seminary. Organic gardens and environmental healing could be part of the monastery's ministry in the city, connecting theory with practice in the neighborhood. Students could live in community in households in the neighborhood.

While seminaries can and should respond to the need for theological education for the new monasticism, other options could be developed in the interim. Through partnerships with the Christian Community Development Association, the Schools for Conversion, and the Upper Room, the United Methodist Church could develop a fine program to equip clergy and lay persons to live in new monastic communities. The resources to prepare people to answer this kind of call are all around us. We simply need to be creative, pro-active, and be willing to "cast our nets to the other side."

SIX

Reports from the Horizon

Truly we are at the beginning of a new day in Methodism, one that is marked by faithful disciples of all ages and every kind of diversity, forming micro-communities of prayer and action. In this chapter we present three emerging expressions of new monasticism within United Methodism. These grassroots examples are not the only communities that are forming, but they are sufficiently representative, we believe, to ignite the imagination of our sisters and brothers who are longing for spring. These are not examples to be slavishly imitated, or to be franchised in some way. They are works in progress, thus there is no guarantee of their longevity over the centuries to come. Yet even in their newness and still-forming identities, these new monastic communities can serve as icons, windows through which we may see divine love calling us to holiness of heart and life.

The first expression is an old fashioned Wesley band meeting that has been in existence for more than six years at Wesley Theological Seminary, shaping the lives of students and faculty alike. Scott has been a member of the band from its inception. The second example is from William Thiele whose School for Contemplative Living in New Orleans is the beginning of what we expect will become a network of various expressions of new monasticism, in due time. The final example is New Day, a growing network of new monastic communities in the Dallas/Ft. Worth metroplex. Elaine and two of her former students, Nathanial Hearne and Richard Newton, are the "instigators" of New Day (a term bestowed on them by Doug Pagitt).

BAND MEETINGS NOW

I (Scott) had heard of band meetings through my study of Methodist history, and had been in covenant discipleship groups in seminary and in various ministry settings. However, until I came to Wesley Theological Seminary as instructor in evangelism, I had never known of a band meeting in practice. The band I am now part of began about six years before I came to Wesley. The summer after her first year in seminary, a student had had a conversion experience. The following fall she and a number of other students, independent of each other, came to Doug Strong, professor of Church History, seeking fellowship. Six people, both men and women, then agreed to meet together as a class meeting with Dr. Strong.

After two years, most of the original group graduated from the seminary. Those who remained all happened to be men. The group then decided to adopt the band meeting format, using the five questions, and be more intentional about pushing each other towards greater accountability.

I was invited to join the band in 2002, a couple of months after I had arrived on campus. I was intimidated at first. A professor (especially a new professor) confessing sins to students seemed at best awkward and perhaps dangerous. I wasn't sure I could be honest. That was four years ago. What I found was that "no temptation has seized [me] except what is common."

After one of us confesses, someone speaks words of assurance, such as, "if we confess our sins, God is faithful and just to forgive us our sins, and cleanse us from all unrighteousness." I never knew the truth of those words experientially until being part of this group.

Various students have come and gone. What has remained constant is God's work our lives, gradually freeing us for obedience in one area, while showing us where we are still in bondage.

About a year ago, I learned about another band meeting in the Baltimore-Washington Annual Conference. A young clergy, and Wesley graduate, Daniel Mejia, was helping me as a teaching assistant. We discovered we each attended band meetings. While at seminary, Mejia had been looking for spiritual direction. His roommate introduced him to Rev. Dennis Dorsch. After two years of private spiritual direction, Mejia was invited to join a band that had been started by Rev. Dorsch with others who had come to him for direction. In that band, members commit to a covenant of daily exercise, Bible reading, journaling, and prayer for each other. Neglecting the covenant is considered "sin" for the purposes of confession. They meet weekly, study the lectionary, and then confess, using the five band questions.

"I would probably not be in ministry, if it weren't for the support and the accountability we get," says Mejia. "Support goes both ways. It challenges us to be pushed when we don't want to do things or we think we can't. It supports us when we need help, when we are attacked and confused. . . . I really don't know how pastors can function by themselves."

WILLIAM THIELE AND NEW MONASTICISM IN NEW ORLEANS[1]

The School for Contemplative Living in New Orleans, Louisiana, was created by Rayne UMC and Parker UMC to practice the integration of contemplative living and serving. We are becoming an ecumenical "monastery without walls," and a form of the new monasticism which cultivates prayerful presence for God as we serve with the world around us in this post-Katrina city. We offer daily, weekly, and monthly opportunities to gather in community, and invite persons from around the country to come stay with us for awhile as we all seek to learn how to balance the *inward journey* towards God's presence with the *outward journey* into the wild life of service around us.

You can learn more about us by contacting the founding spiritual director, Rev. William E. Thiele, PhD, at soulcare4u@bellsouth.net and by going to the website at www.thescl.net. Beth Morgan, a member of our SCL community, wrote the following description of life among us:

> As a contemplative, I'm drawn inward, to seek and know God's presence in the stillness at the very center of being. Within the quiet inner space, I wait, watch, and listen as Presence moves and speaks. There, I surrender to the transformative work of God Within and learn to love and to be loved by God. It is a solitary and personal journey, and, for a time, I thought it (the solitary journey) was what was meant by "the contemplative life." But I've been moved to join contemplatives in community at the School

1. The information in this section was provided by William Thiele and a member of his community, Beth Morgan.

for Contemplative Living (SCL) in New Orleans, Louisiana, and to reach out to others in service with that community. I've learned that being in community strengthens my individual spiritual practice and enriches my contemplative life.

By participating in centering prayer groups and retreats at SCL, I've learned new ways to experience God. I have, at times, been awestruck by the interconnectedness of the group and by God's unitive presence among us. Friends in the community offer steadying hands and hearts; help me open to, and accept, all that I am; sit with me and teach me to sit; and remind me of the absolute joy of being here. The community also helps keep my solitary practice from becoming self-centered and self-gratifying.

The interactions and activities of SCL members help each of us become better at listening and sharing, giving and taking, and supporting and being supported, so that we can be more skillful in reaching out to people beyond our contemplative community. At SCL, there are many opportunities to serve. Community leadership is shared and members give their time and gifts in areas such as teaching, art, music, writing, service, and hospitality. SCL has encouraged me as I write a contemplative blog that offers support and encouragement to people from our community and around the world.[2]

Through SCL, I'm also learning to serve the homeless in New Orleans. Serving at the intersection where the deep interior heart and the exterior world meet is not an easy or comfortable place, but I can't help others see and hear and experience God unless I'm willing to help meet their physical needs and work to mitigate injustices. SCL's motto is "listening in stillness, serving in joy." By serving with the community, I'm learning to meet practical needs, to be respectful and offer hospitality to people living on the edge of society, to practice stillness and right action, to be peaceful in the midst of chaos, to be pushed and not push back, to be love in the face of resentment and anger. By serving with SCL, I'm able to work from a still and centered heart and to listen to God's whispered direction and guidance. I'm learning to respond to God's presence in my life by loving God *and* loving my neighbor with all of my being. I'm learning to follow Jesus' path.

2. See the blog titled "Walking in Wonder: Notes from a Contemplative Path." Online: http://quiet1.wordpress.com/.

THE PEOPLE OF NEW DAY

New Day is a new form of Methodism that is grounded in the original Wesleyan vision for spreading scriptural holiness across the land. We are micro-communities of prayer and action. We follow a Wesleyan rule of life that is structured around the United Methodist membership vows (prayer, presence, gifts, service, and witness), and that is influenced by Wesley's General Rules. While we believe New Day communities can be formed in any context, we are working to develop them especially in financially disadvantaged communities, both urban and rural. We are committed to a Wesleyan vision of holiness that integrates a disciplined life of prayer with prophetic and healing action in the world around us. We believe that this form of evangelistic presence is deeply faithful to Methodist theology and to the best of our Methodist tradition. Our communities are led by teams of three or more people, clergy or lay, who are theologically equipped for this form of ministry. Our community leaders are bi-vocational and our communities meet in homes or other borrowed space. These two practices free us to use our financial resources for mission, and provide us with great flexibility in terms of where we meet.

Our first New Day community was born in the summer of 2008 on the campus of Southern Methodist University, with a handful of Perkins students, SMU students, and a motley crew of others. Our goal in forming the first New Day community at SMU, was to create a context where students (undergraduates, graduate students, and Perkins students) and others could participate in this form of Methodism with its rule of life, team leadership, missional ecclesiology, and emergent worship gathering. We believed that it was especially important to inspire the imagination of young adults in this form of Methodism because they will carry the DNA into the future in diverse settings whether they serve God through ordained or lay ministry. New Day SMU is a kind of "incubator" for preparing others to start New Day communities elsewhere. That is its primary mission.

We partnered with the Wesley Foundation and the campus chaplain's office in order to support their existing ministries. (We believe in collaboration rather than competition in the church.) New Day SMU meets for worship in the Wesley Foundation house on Sunday evenings, 5:00–7:00

PM. Our lead team for 2009–2010 includes six people: two Perkins students (one of whom is our intern), two seminary professors (one is professor emeritus), the Wesley Foundation director, and one undergraduate, a senior who is planning to go to seminary after he graduates. In keeping with our rule of life, our lead team is diverse in terms of race, gender, and age.

We begin our worship gathering with a simple meal of soup and bread that we take turns providing. We then move into our worship, which is multi-sensory and highly participatory. Our worship includes ancient liturgies, diverse forms of music, silence, and weekly communion. The preaching is creative and emergent, shared by the lead team and with occasional guest preachers. We are fiercely multi-generational and include children in worship leadership and all aspects of our community life.

In the summer of 2009 we began a community garden in order to help students learn about environmental justice and community transformation through urban agriculture, in keeping with our rule of life. We have plans to begin working with already existing United Methodist ministries to incarcerated persons and homeless persons in the coming year so that students have opportunities to learn to serve in areas of great social and spiritual need.

With the encouragement and support of the North Texas Conference, we now have funding for more Perkins interns to help us start and develop more New Day communities. Several churches around and beyond the Metroplex are now in various stages of preparation and planning to start New Day communities that will be anchored in their churches. This means that they are preparing leaders who will develop and lead New Day communities that are satellite congregations of established United Methodist churches.

In some cases these New Day communities will be congregations with collegial ties to the anchor church. This is especially true for New Day communities whose lead teams include bi-vocational clergy (New Day SMU enjoys a collegial tie to Lovers Lane UMC). In other cases, especially when the communities are led by theologically equipped lay leaders, New Day members may attend worship at the anchor church on Sunday, but their ministry will be their missional and spiritual formation ministry in the neighborhoods of the New Day members.

We believe that the formation of New Day communities that partner with Wesley Foundations hold special potential for bringing renewal to the UMC, and missional presence to a hurting world, because through campus New Day communities students can learn to live and minister according to the New Day rule of life. Their vocational self-understanding can be shaped by the New Day ethos, and they will carry that DNA into the future. We also believe that students are hungry for this form of church.

To provide students with an even more focused experience of living in intentional community and following a rule of life while practicing hospitality with their neighbors, the Epworth Project was born. In July, 2008, a donor from New Day provided a house, rent free other than utilities, in a mixed income, predominantly working poor neighborhood in Garland. Three Perkins students live there in intentional community, following a Wesleyan rule of life together, and practicing hospitality in the neighborhood of the house. These students participate in the New Day community. One of the Epworth scholars is serving her internship with New Day and the Wesley Foundation in the coming year.

During the summer of 2009, a second Epworth Project house, the Bonhoeffer House, was founded for students and one of our team leaders for the New Day community in Euless/Hurst. A third house is hosted by a multi-generational family in a beautiful rural setting just outside Kaufman, Texas. The family who owns the Kaufman house is part of the newly forming New Day community in Kaufman. In all these cases the donors continue to own the houses, but allow the community members to live there rent free, other than utilities. Students sign a lease as they would for any rental property. They also sign a covenant for living in the house in community. Students apply for an Epworth Scholarship as they would for any other scholarship.

THE NEW DAY RULE OF LIFE

Prayers
- We will pray daily
- We will use a variety of forms of prayer such as the reflective reading of Scripture and other spiritual texts, confession, the prayer of examen, intercession, journaling, and contemplation
- We will fast from food once a week (either a full or partial fast)

Presence
- We will practice a contemplative stance in order to be present to God, the world, and ourselves
- We will be hospitable to our neighbors in our families, neighborhoods and workplaces
- We will be hospitable to our faith community through participation in our worship, fellowship and mission

Gifts
- We will honor and care for the gift of the earth and its resources, practicing ecologically responsible living, striving for simplicity rather than excessive consumption
- We will practice generosity in sharing our material resources, including money, within and beyond this community
- We will use our spiritual gifts, talents and abilities to serve God within and beyond this community

Service
- We will serve God and neighbor out of gratitude for the love of God
- We will practice mutual accountability with a covenant group within the community, for how we serve God and neighbor
- We will practice regular Sabbath as a means of renewal so that we can lovingly serve God and neighbor

Witness
- We will practice racial and gender reconciliation
- We will resist evil and injustice
- We will pursue peace with justice
- We will share the redeeming, healing, creative love of God in word, deed and presence as an invitation to others to experience the transforming love of God.

> *I commit to this rule of life and to the well-being of this community, out of gratitude to God who forgives, heals, and makes all things new. May my life be a blessing within and beyond God's church, for the transformation of the world.*

CONCLUSION

When speaking about new monasticism in local churches I (Elaine) am often asked if these little communities can really make much of a difference in light of the massive challenges to the church today. I am also asked whether I think the new communities will survive beyond a few short years. The risk of failure in new communities, after all, is high, regardless of the kind of community. These questions bring to mind a comment from a young man I met recently in the U.K., Ben Brown. Ben and his wife Ru are second generation members of the Northumbria Community.

We were walking with a group of students on a short pilgrimage to St. Cuthbert's cave, then to the top of a low hill so that we could see the Holy Island of Lindisfarne. As we rested along the way, Ben said that in the U.K. his generation of new monastics are keenly aware of their country's history of imperialism, and the way empire has deformed Christianity in the west. Thus they are averse to any kind of empire building in the name of new monasticism. He said they hope to be faithful to God and to love their neighbor now, this week, this year, but they do not worry about whether their little community will create a lasting legacy or a new order that will be around until the eschaton. Squinting against a cobalt sky, the Holy Island of Lindisfarne at his back, Ben smiled, "We leave the future to God."

May we learn to do the same. For the real questions are not "Will these Methodist new monastic communities last until the Lord comes back? Will they produce financial resources for our connectional system? Will new monastic leaders who want to be ordained, be willing to leave intentional community so that they can itinerate?" The real question is, "What is the Spirit saying to the church?"

Recommended Resources for Further Study

While this book has focused on developing new monastic communities within the United Methodist tradition, many other excellent resources are available for further study. Some of them have to do with monasticism in general, both new and old. Others are oriented toward certain practices of new monasticism. A few that we recommend are from the emerging church conversation but have been included because they help us to understand cultural changes that are creating a context in which new monasticism has emerged. While reading about new monasticism opens one's eyes to possibilities for new expressions of Wesleyan community, nothing can replace a visit in order to experience the heart and soul of a community. Thus we recommend getting to know some of the communities first hand. No two are alike. We have described several in this book. To find out more about locations of other communities and contact information, visit http://www.communityofcommunities.us.

The following books have been organized using the authors' last names in alphabetical order:

Bessenecker, Scott A. *The New Friars: The Emerging Movement Serving the World's Poor.* **Downer's Grove, IL: InterVarsity, 2006.**

"The New Monasticism, as it is being called, often consists of households of Christian men and women planted in dying inner-city communities within their home country, attempting to live the Christian ideal among their neighbors, drawing the lost, poor and broken to themselves. They resemble more the cloistered order. The new friars, on the other hand, have something of the spirit of mission-driven monks and nuns in them, leaving their mother country and moving to those parts of the world where little is known about Jesus."[1]

In this book, Scott A. Bessenecker introduces an array of "new friars," mostly evangelical in their faith traditions, who have answered God's call to serve among the poorest of the poor in slums, ghettoes, dumps, and villages around the world. Unlike Catholic friars and nuns serving the poor, these men and women are sometimes married and do not necessarily practice a severe asceticism in their personal lives, other than choosing to live among the poor.

As might be expected, Bessenecker provides significant insight into the causes of global poverty, offering pointed reflection on the impact of Walmart and other transnational corporations on impoverished countries. Using many stories from the lives and ministries of the new friars, the author helps readers understand how unchecked consumerism in wealthy nations causes appalling poverty in the rest of the world. It is painful to read the stories of human suffering, yet this book is deeply inspiring, a celebration of the faithfulness and joy of the new friars and their work.

Bonhoeffer, Dietrich. *Life Together*. Translated and with an Introduction by John W. Doberstein. New York: HarperSanFrancisco, 1954.

This book is the classic text on life in community, written by the German Lutheran theologian, Dietrich Bonhoeffer (1906–1945), who coined the phrase, "a new kind of monasticism." Bonhoeffer was martyred by the Gestapo because of his participation in a plot to assassinate Hitler. Just a few days after he was put to death in the concentration camp at Flossenburg, the camp was liberated by allied forces. A member of the Confessing Church, Bonhoeffer became the leader of an underground seminary at Finkenwalde. There he lived in community with twenty-five vicars. *Life Together* was written partly as an account of life in that community, and partly as a meditation for others who wish to live in community.

---

1. Bessenecker, *New Friars*, 21–22.

Foundational for new monasticism, this book lays out clear, practical advice for creating a truly Christian community, for following a daily office, for practicing ministry, and for confession and communion. In addition to the Bible and graduate work in systematic theology, Bonhoeffer was influenced by Ghandi, as well as Richard and Reinhold Niebuhr. During his year at Union Theological Seminary in New York, he was deeply moved by the African American struggle for equality.

"Let him who cannot be alone beware of community,"[2] Bonhoeffer writes in the section on practicing solitude and silence. Community requires self knowledge and inner work, and the capacity to listen to the Word of God in silence. Likewise, "Let him who is not in community beware of being alone." We are never truly alone because Jesus is always with us, as is the communion of the saints, even when we do not feel their presence. Thus for Bonhoeffer a contemplative stance is essential to living in community.

The practice of intercessory prayer is described as the most powerful way to heal divisions between people, an essential ingredient in community. Through intercession we see the other's offensiveness through new eyes, because ". . . everything in him that repels us falls away, we see him in all his destitution and need. His need and his sin become so heavy and oppressive that we feel them as our own, and we can do nothing else but pray."[3] Within community, intercession is every Christian's responsibility and privilege, especially for the pastor.[4]

Life Together is essential reading for all who feel called to new monasticism.

Claiborne, Shane. *Irresistible Revolution: Living as an Ordinary Radical*. Grand Rapids: Zondervan, 2006.

Perhaps more than anyone else, Shane Claiborne has inspired scores of Christians to embrace the new monasticism. This book is Claiborne's story of how he became involved in ministry among homeless people in Philadelphia, leading him to found the Simple Way community with a few

2. Bonhoeffer, *Life Together*, 77.
3. Ibid., 86.
4. Ibid., 87–88.

friends. Claiborne has become a household name in many churches as he has responded to invitations across the nation to speak in all manner of churches, colleges, and youth functions. Everywhere he goes he preaches a simple message that every Christian has the potential to live as an "ordinary radical" for Jesus.

"Jesus wrecked my life," he writes, with gentle humor. "The more I read the gospel, the more it messed me up, turning everything I believed in, valued, and hoped for upside-down. I am still recovering from my conversion."[5] Unlike the typical "Damascus Road" conversion story common among evangelicals, with a rotten sinner turning to Jesus and cleaning up his life, Claiborne was a clean cut prom king, smart and popular in high school. When Jesus exposed him to the poverty and need of people as a college student, he could no longer pursue the American dream.[6] He was unable to reconcile the Jesus of much of American churchdom with the Jesus of the Gospels. "I decided that one of the best ways to discover the historical Jesus is to deconstruct the American totem, to take him off the totem pole we have nailed him to."[7]

Claiborne's journey included time spent at Willow Creek, one of the nation's first mega-churches, as well as time in Calcutta where he learned from Mother Teresa. The problem with most American middle class Christians, according to Claiborne, is not ignorance of poverty, but absence of relationships with the poor. "I had come to see that the great tragedy in the church is not that rich Christians do not care about the poor but that rich Christians do not know the poor."[8]

Often, Christians with a prophetic message like Claiborne's are strident, difficult to hear. But Claiborne is a master at disarming his audience through humor. He is well informed theologically and has done his homework on church history. His goal is to help ordinary Christians become "extremists for love." Writing in a post-9/11 climate of fear, Claiborne says that "if terror is the enemy, then love is the hero."[9] Saul of Tarsus was the first terrorist who targeted Christians, he reminds readers. "Scandalous

---

5. Claiborne, *Irresistible Revolution*, 41.
6. Ibid., 42.
7. Ibid., 113.
8. Ibid.
9. Ibid., 271.

grace," not violence, converted Saul to Jesus.[10] Surely as the church becomes filled with that spirit of grace, many more Sauls will come into the fold.

Claiborne believes that getting smaller is the solution to the problem of the church's loss of mission. Through the development of communities of disciples who follow Jesus and love their neighbors, the church will come home to its God-given identity.[11] *Irresistible Revolution* does not provide nuts and bolts directions for how to develop a community, how to train leaders, or how to relate the community effectively to an anchor church. What it does do is call forth from readers a willingness to follow Jesus in the way of the gospel.

Claiborne, Shane, and Jonathan Wilson-Hartgrove. *Becoming the Answer to Our Prayers: Prayer for Ordinary Radicals.* **Downer's Grove, IL: InterVarsity, 2008.**

In this book, Shane Claiborne and Jonathan Wilson-Hartgrove team up to talk about the necessity of grounding new monasticism in a life of prayer and the church, rather than in activism. While affirming social justice activism as an essential part of living in the kingdom of God, the authors wisely point readers to Jesus's example in the New Testament. Three prayers shape their discourse: the Lord's Prayer, John 17, and Eph 1:15–23. The prayers become a framework for thinking about how to pray and how to live the new monastic life.

Claiborne and Wilson-Hartgrove gained their hard-won wisdom from living and working in areas with devastating poverty and its attendant social problems. They know that burnout is guaranteed if their inner life is not sustained through prayer.

Burnout is not the only danger. Temptation is a constant problem for new monastics just as it is for everyone else. "Sometimes people ask us if we are scared, living in the inner city. We usually reply with something like "We're more afraid of shopping malls" . . . While the ghettos may have their share of violence and crime, the posh suburbs are home to more

10. Ibid., 272.

11. Ibid., 322–23.

subtle demonic forces—numbness, complacency, and comfort. These are the powers that can eat away at our souls."[12]

While some of the anecdotes in this book are repeats of stories in their other books, this book is still very helpful in linking a sustained life of prayer that is grounded in Scripture and tradition, to sustained and fruitful new monastic ministry.

Cole, Neil. *Organic Church: Growing Faith Where Life Happens*. San Francisco: Jossey-Bass, 2005.

This is not a book about new monasticism, but about a related phenomenon that Neil Cole calls organic church. Within six years, at the time of writing this book, Cole and his associate had planted nearly 800 churches "in thirty two states and twenty three nations around the world."[13] The churches are very simple expanding networks of micro-communities that meet in homes, coffee shops, restaurants, and other places. Cole describes these locations as "smoking sections," the kinds of places that the established church has not considered as appropriate places for new faith communities. "If you want to win this world to Christ, you are going to have to sit in the smoking section. That is where lost people are found, and if you make them put their cigarette out to hear the message they will be thinking about only one thing: "When can I get another cigarette?"[14]

As is the case with new monastics, Cole and his colleagues believe the church needs to leave its cloistered comfort inside a church building and take the community of God out into the broken places of the world. A strength of Cole's position is his emphasis on the kingdom of God rather than denominationalism, in sharing the gospel.

Cole refers to leadership development as "farming." In his plan every Christian is to be cultivated into a missional Christian who shares his or her faith in their realms of influence, organically.[15] New communities start as soon as leaders are ready to lead them. While he writes with passion about disciple formation rather than gathering "members" into the

12. Claiborne and Wilson-Hartgrove, *Becoming the Answer to Our Prayers*, 53.
13. Cole, *Organic Church*, 26.
14. Ibid., xxvii.
15. Ibid., 205.

church, his network of organic churches seem less connected to the rest of the church than is the case with the best of new monasticism.

The gift of this book to a study of new monasticism is that it helps to explain the cultural realities of the church in a post-denominational, post-Christendom era. Its model of networks of micro-communities also helps us to envision a network of new monastic communities grounded in the same anchor church.

Halter, Hugh, and Matt Smay. *The Tangible Kingdom: Creating Incarnational Community.* San Francisco: Jossey-Bass, 2008.

Hugh Halter and Matt Smay have written a compelling account of the formation of "incarnational community" in a typical suburban neighborhood in Colorado, which led to a network of communities and eventually a training program. Many of their insights and principles are consistent with the new monasticism. What makes their approach different is that they are writing especially for middle class, suburban American Christians who long to live a new monastic kind of life but have not been called to move to a poor neighborhood.

Essentially, their model involves becoming hospitable in the neighborhood where you live, forming real friendships with the people there, and in the context of journeying with those friends and neighbors, introduce them to the kingdom of God. The authors come from a conservative evangelical background, so some of their struggles to live into the tangible kingdom are connected with developing a lived ecclesiology that is focused on the kingdom rather than on doctrine, though doctrine matters.

The writing style is simple and readable, frequently punctuated with humor. One of the most helpful paradigms the authors present is a set of four principles necessary in order for the church to be the tangible kingdom of God. These are leaving, listening, living among, and loving without strings attached, with a chapter devoted to each. There are "enemies" to these four aspects of kingdom life. "Selfishness is the enemy of Leaving. Fear is the enemy of Living Among. Arrogance is the enemy of Listening. Expectations are the enemy of Loving."[16] These four practices and their

16. Halter and Smay, *Tangible Kingdom*, 144.

"enemies" are especially helpful for United Methodists to consider in the establishment of new monastic communities.

Heath, Elaine A. *The Mystic Way of Evangelism: A Contemplative Vision for Christian Outreach*. Grand Rapids: Baker Academic, 2008.

In this book I describe the church in the United States entering a dark night of the soul, classically understood. The way to move through the night to a new day of missional health, is to let go of programmatic approaches to mission and evangelism, and to take up a kenotic life. The guides for our journey through the night are the saints, mystics, and martyrs of the church. Their lives and writings teach us what we need to know about evangelism in the post-Christendom west.

The first part of the book, "Purgation," describes the contemporary situation in the church in terms of decline, financial struggle, and loss of moral authority in the eyes of a watching world. Included in this section are comments about decline in the United Methodist Church.

The second part of the book, "Illumination," presents five themes that will characterize the church of the future, one that lives in a contemplative stance. Each theme is presented through the stories and teaching of two great Christian mystics. The selection of mystics was intentionally diverse in terms of Christian faith traditions, race, and gender. One of the mystics, Phoebe Palmer, was a Methodist.

The third part of the book casts a vision for one possible model of a church that incarnates the themes presented in Part Two. This is done through narrative theology, with a fictitious character named Sam who is gradually evangelized through his relationship with a congregation (First Church) that is living in a contemplative stance. First Church is a mainline church that is a new monastic community with a team of bi-vocational pastors. It is written in a way that takes into account the Episcopal system and United Methodist polity.

The Mystic Way of Evangelism takes seriously the challenges and decline in the church as we know it, yet it points to the mysterious activity of the Holy Spirit in calling the church to move through the night not with despair, but with hope.

Hirsch, Allan. *The Forgotten Ways: Reactivating the Missional Church.*
Grand Rapids: Brazos Press, 2006.

This is a powerful, essential book for those who are called to move out of
the comfortable familiarity of church as usual, into vital, missional life in
God's kingdom. Allan Hirsch is the founding director of Forge Mission
Training Network in Australia. Drawing from the two great missionary
movements in the history of the church—the early church and the underground church in twentieth-century China, Hirsch enumerates the
changes that must take place in order for the church to become missional
once again.

The missional church, according to Hirsch, is much more like Al
Qaeda than what we think of as church. The reason the early church and
the Chinese underground church have flourished despite heavy persecution, is that the structure made it impossible to "take them out."[17] By
decentralizing leadership, location, and training, and doing ministry bi-
vocationally rather than as a paid profession, the church is able to spread
"virus-like" in even the most inhospitable locations.

Hirsch identifies a fivefold model of church DNA that he believes is
latent in every believer and every church. The missional church must be
characterized by these five expressions of ministry and leadership. APEPT,
the acronym for the model, stands for: apostolic, prophetic, evangelistic,
pastoral, and teaching.[18] When these five are functioning in a healthy way,
a church cannot help but be missional.

One of the great strengths Hirsch brings to this book is his expertise
in missiology. In a section in which he describes "incarnational mission,"
Hirsch critiques the imposition of the missionaries' cultures upon those
being evangelized. Having already discussed the tragedy of the Guarani in
South America (whose story was made famous in the movie, *The Mission*),
Hirsch writes:

> By way of contrast we have distorted the meaning of incarnational
> mission when as Western missionaries we have imposed fledged
> denominational templates on Third World nations. Not only does
> this diminish the validity of local culture, but it alienates the lo-

17. Hirsch, *Forgotten Ways*, 205–6.
18. Ibid., 170–71.

cal Christians from their cultural surroundings by transposing a Western Cultural expression in the place of local ones. The net result is a poor black man in the middle of the bush in Africa, dressed in robes and standing outside of a gothic style church building, calling people to worship in ways that barely make sense even to the cultures that started them. In these cases no attempt is made to contextualize (localize) either Gospel or church, and yet we wonder why these have little lasting effect on the surrounding populations. While the error is easier to spot in the middle of Africa, we do the same thing all across the now highly tribalized West.[19]

Hirsch helps readers understand our own neighborhoods as missionary contexts, and with the insight of a missiologist maps out "the forgotten ways" of holistic evangelism that are what the world needs today.

Rutba House, editor. *School(s) for Conversion: 12 Marks of a New Monasticism.* Eugene, OR: Cascade, 2005.

This little gem is the textbook for the Schools for Conversion, the introduction to new monasticism. Edited by the Rutba House, including Jonathan Wilson-Hartgrove, the book includes essays by twelve practitioners of new monasticism. In June 2004, a conference was held in Durham, NC, for people across the United States who are involved in new expressions of monasticism. Participants hoped to identify common forms of life that marked their communities regardless of denominational background, gender, age, and other variables. By the end of the conference attendees had identified twelve "marks" of the new monasticism. While every community did not have every mark, these features were widely present across the board.

The Schools for Conversion were developed out of this original conference, as a way to complement other forms of theological education with contextualized formation in the ways of new monasticism. Today there are several schools held every year around the nation and in South America.

Since the Schools for Conversion were already described (along with the twelve marks) in chapter 5, no more will be said about them here. This

19. Ibid., 137.

book is a good introduction to the basic precepts of new monasticism, written by a very diverse array of practitioners.

Sine, Tom. *The New Conspirators: Creating the Future One Mustard Seed at a Time.* Downer's Grove, IL: InterVarsity, 2008.

According to Tom Sine there are four major creative streams in the church today: Emerging, Missional, Mosaic, and Monastic. In this book he traces the "new conspirators" who are leading communities and mission in these four streams. It is a "mustard seed conspiracy" of Christians who are willing to pioneer ancient/future forms of church in diverse social contexts around the world.

The book is organized into conversations (topics) that take seriously the new conspirators despite their work in the margins, the globalized, post-9/11 cultures in which we live, the future of God which brings transformation to this world, the turbulent economic times in which we live, and the need for our imaginations to be reshaped by the gospel.

A masterful and hopeful expert on global trends, Sine has traveled extensively around the world to learn about emergence on every continent. His book is filled with stories of faithful Christians who are pioneering new forms of Christian community. One of the gifts of this book to the new monasticism is that he helps to contextualize it globally in relationship to political, economic, environmental, and ecclesiological realities. As a seventy-something Episcopalian with a commitment to the well being of God's church, Sine offers a much-needed voice of encouragement and gratitude to the new conspirators.

Stock, Jon, Tim Otto, and Jonathan Wilson-Hartgrove. *Inhabiting the Church: Biblical Wisdom for a New Monasticism.* Eugene, OR: Cascade, 2006.

The three authors of this book offer an evangelical analysis of the Rule of St. Benedict in order to recommend the practices of Benedictine spirituality for new monasticism. *Inhabiting the Church* is used for a textbook for Schools for Conversion that focuses on spiritual practices to nurture life in new monastic communities.

The book is especially helpful for readers who are from a free church, evangelical background in which monasticism is a somewhat foreign, "Catholic" concept. Many people who come to new monasticism are unfamiliar with the long history of monasticism. Often they do not know about St. Benedict, the father of monasticism in the West, nor do they necessarily have a grounding in the spiritual disciplines common to monastic life. With a spirituality shaped by the Bible, it is important for these Christians to learn about the scriptural grounding for monastic practices.

In this book the authors introduce and reflect upon the vows of Benedictine monasticism: conversion, obedience, and stability. Well-written and well-researched, this is a readable, concise guide for communities to know how to invite Benedictine spirituality to shape their life together.

Tickle, Phyllis. *The Great Emergence: How Christianity Is Changing and Why.* Grand Rapids: Baker, 2008.

Phyllis Tickle has become something of an icon for emerging Christians. Like Tom Sine, she comes to the conversation from the Episcopal tradition and is an internationally known authority on religion and religious trends. She is the founding editor of the Religion Department of *Publishers Weekly.*

In this book Tickle provides a broad introduction to the history of emergence in the church. Citing Anglican Bishop Mark Dyer, Tickle states that every five hundred years the church has a giant rummage sale, where some things that used to work are gotten rid of, as new forms of church emerge. "That is, as Bishop Dyer observes, about every five hundred years the empowered structures of institutionalized Christianity, whatever they may be at that time, become an intolerable carapace that must be shattered in order that renewal and new growth may occur."[20] Whenever a five hundred year rummage sale takes place, writes Tickle, there are always three results. A new form of Christianity emerges that is alive and fruitful. The previously dominant form of Christianity is "reconstituted into a more pure and less ossified version of itself,"[21] and a fresh outpouring

20. Tickle, *Great Emergence*, 16.
21. Ibid., 17.

of evangelistic power takes place in both the emerging form of church and the cleansed, established form. Unfortunately there is also a history of violence during these times as the established form of church resists and attempts to stop the emergence from happening.

Tickle describes how the five hundred year rummage sales (times of Great Emergence) are bound together with breakthroughs in communication and information technologies, politics, and economics. The last rummage sale was during the time of the Protestant Reformations. What the church is undergoing now is another Great Emergence.

Readable and often witty, this book helps readers understand from an historic perspective why the church is undergoing such upheaval today, and why the massive cultural shifts in which we live are actually ushering in new, vital forms of church that are Spirit breathed. This is ultimately a hopeful and enlightening book, one that everyone who is interested in emergence and new monasticism should read.

Wilson-Hartgrove, Jonathan. *To Baghdad and Beyond: How I Got Born Again in Babylon*. Eugene, OR: Cascade, 2005.

This is the story of the founding of Rutba House, the community of Jonathan and Leah Wilson-Hartgrove in Walltown, an historic black neighborhood of Durham, North Carolina. At the beginning of the war in Iraq Wilson-Hartgrove and some friends traveled to Iraq in hopes of communicating to the Iraqi people an American message of peace and goodwill. At the time the Wilson-Hartgroves were part of the Mennonite Church, which is a pacifist denomination. Having come from a Southern Baptist beginning, this was Jonathan's initiation into "the third way" of Jesus's non-violent resistance to evil.

The pivotal event in the lives of the Wilson-Hartgroves and their friends was when a car accident nearly took their friends' lives on the road outside of Baghdad. Responding quickly to the emergency, some Muslim doctors and nurses created a makeshift clinic in the nearby village of Rutba, saving the lives of the Wilson-Hartgrove's friends. The real hospital had been destroyed by American bombs. This experience of Iraqi compassion and hospitality left a permanent mark on the Wilson-Hartgroves and their friends. When they subsequently founded their community in

Walltown, they named it Rutba House out of gratitude for the love and kindness they had experienced in Rutba, Iraq.

This event was part of what led Jonathan and Leah Wilson-Hartgrove into the new monasticism. One of the twelve marks of the new monasticism is peacemaking in the midst of violence and conflict resolution along the lines of Matthew 18. Through their experiences in modern Babylon (Iraq is the site of the ancient city of Babylon), a new understanding was born of their own vocations and of possibilities for the future of the church.

Wilson-Hartgrove, Jonathan. *New Monasticism: What it Has to Say to Today's Church.* **Grand Rapids: Brazos, 2008.**

In some ways this is Jonathan's most important work for introducing new monasticism to the church, because it explains how and why new monastic communities must remain connected to the rest of the church in order to fulfill their vocation. With his trademark conversational writing style, the author traces the rise of new monasticism in the Bible and in history, gives an overview of new monastic emphases, and explains why new monastics need the church. For United Methodists who are drawn to new monasticism this book can be especially helpful.

Wilson-Hartgrove, Jonathan. *Free to Be Bound: Church Beyond the Color Line.* **Colorado Springs, CO: NavPress, 2008.**

There is a common saying that the most segregated place in the world is the church at 11 o'clock Sunday morning. In this volume Jonathan focuses on racial reconciliation as a major focus of new monasticism, and why the church must become sensitized to its participation in the deep racial divisions that perpetuate injustice in our world. This is a prophetic work that is essential reading for new monastics and the church at large.

This list of fifteen books is just a beginning. Many others could be included, though they do not focus exclusively on new monasticism. The work of Brian McLaren, for example, is helpful in understanding emergent contexts and questions, and represents an emerging position that is strongly oriented toward social justice. Alan Hirsch has written several other important and pertinent books, as have Tom Sine and Phyllis Tickle. The work of Alan Roxburgh and Darrel Guder in the categories of missional church and missional leadership development are helpful. Tony Jones and Doug Pagitt are among the most popular voices in the emerging church, which though at times diverges significantly from new monasticism, is still part of what Tickle calls the Great Emergence.

Reflection Guide

The reflection guide that follows is intended to be used by small groups for a six week spiritual formation and discernment process. We have included recommended Scripture readings, hymns, reflection questions on each chapter, and movies with pertinent themes to help readers engage as fully as possible, the issues that are raised in this book. Additional activities could include a field trip to visit a new monastic community in your area, if possible, and/or a traditional monastery (Benedictine or otherwise). Another potentially rich activity would be to ride a bus through disadvantaged areas of your city, if public transportation is available. Become familiar with the abandoned places of empire where you live.

To gain the maximum potential from this reflection guide we suggest that readers assemble in a small group such as a church leadership team or a few friends who are interested in new monasticism, and work through this book together over a period of six weeks. (This would be a fine Lenten study.) Each week individuals should do all the readings and as many recommended activities as possible. Once a week the group should gather to process what individuals have learned and experienced through the readings, movies, and reflection questions. An outline for a weekly meeting is suggested below. Used in this way, this book could become the beginning of a discernment process for your congregation to develop new monastic ministries.

SCHEDULE FOR WEEKLY GROUP MEETING

- Simple meal such as soup, bread, and dessert prepared by members of the group and preferably served in a group member's home

- Prayer

- Sing the hymn for the week

- Read the Scripture for the week responsively

- If you wish, show a segment from the recommended movie for that week

- Discuss the questions for that week

- Silence for reflection

- Prayer

- Quick review of assignment for week to come, with plans to watch recommended movies or other activities together, when possible

- Unison benediction

ONE

Our Stories

Scripture Reading: Genesis 12:1–8

Hymn: Be Thou My Vision (451, *United Methodist Hymnal*)

Recommended Movie: *The Mission*[22]

For Reflection:
In what ways has the United Methodist Church shaped your spiritual journey?

22. *The Mission*, DVD, directed by Roland Joffé.

What have been the biggest gifts you have received from the United
Methodist Church?

When you read Elaine and Scott's stories, what did you:
    Hope?

    Remember?

    Think?

    Pray?

As you think about the future of the United Methodist Church, what do
you imagine?

When you watched *The Mission*, what did you:
    Hope?

    Remember?

    Think?

    Pray?

Just as God called Abram and Sarai in Genesis 12 to leave their familiar way of life and journey to a new, unknown place, the United Methodist Church is being called into an unknown future. What are the promises and possibilities you see for the UMC as you reflect upon Genesis 12:1–8?

TWO

Early Stories of Intentional Community and Church Renewal

Scripture Reading: Jeremiah 29:11–13

Hymn: Hymn of Promise (707, *United Methodist Hymnal*)

Recommended Movie: *The Secret Life of Bees*[23]

For Reflection:
What are the similarities, if any, between our culture and that of St. Benedict's day?

What might a contemporary, Methodist version of a Beguine community look like for United Methodist women or men living in the suburbs? In an urban setting? In a rural area?

How are early examples of intentional community similar to and different from disciple-making efforts such as Walk to Emmaus or Disciple Bible Studies?

23. *The Secret Life of Bees*, DVD, directed by Gina Prince-Bythewood.

When you watched *The Secret Life of Bees*, what did you:
    Hope?

    Remember?

    Think?

    Pray?

How were the women in *The Secret Life of Bees* like the Benedictines? The Beguines?

Jeremiah 29:11–13 contains a powerful promise for God's people in exile. What is God's promise, and how does it apply to the United Methodist Church? Is the promise of hope and a future unconditional, or are there actions and attitudes that must first be present in order for the promise to be fulfilled?

THREE

Protestant Models of Intentional Community

Scripture Reading: Isaiah 61:1–11

Hymn: O Come, O Come, Emmanuel (211, *United Methodist Hymnal*)

Recommended Movie: *Patch Adams*[24]

24. *Patch Adams*, DVD, directed by Tom Shadyac.

For Reflection:

What are the similarities, if any, between our culture and that of John Wesley's day?

As you read this chapter what did you learn about early Methodism that surprised you?

What are the elements of early Methodism that, if reclaimed, you think would help the United Methodist Church today?

When you watched the movie, *Patch Adams*, what did you:

    Hope?

    Remember?

    Think?

    Pray?

How was Patch Adams like the reformers?

Isaiah 61:1–11 is filled with promises of healing for people who are broken, oppressed, grieved and lonely. As you read through this text slowly, allow the Holy Spirit to bring to your attention a word, phrase or image. As you meditate with that word, phrase, or image, bring the United Methodist Church into your meditation and allow the Holy Spirit to breathe a new prayer into you for the church. In the space below, record your prayer.

FOUR

What the New Methodists Want

Scripture Reading: Luke 9:1–6, 10:1–12

Hymn: Lord, You Give the Great Commission (584, *United Methodist Hymnal*)

Recommended Movie: *Jesus Camp*[25]

For Reflection:
As you read through chapter four, what did you:
    Hope?

    Remember?

    Think?

    Pray?

Why is the word "evangelism" offensive to so many people inside and outside the church?

---

25. *Jesus Camp*, DVD, directed by Heidi Ewing and Rachel Grady.

How can new monasticism change the face of evangelism inside and outside the church?

As you watched the documentary, *Jesus Camp*, what did you:

    Hope?

    Remember?

    Think?

    Pray?

What is the Holy Spirit saying to the United Methodist Church in Luke 9:1–6 and 10:1–12?

FIVE

Spring

Scripture Reading: Acts 2:37–47; 5:12–16

Hymn: One Bread, One Body (620, *United Methodist Hymnal*)

Recommended Movie: *Chocolat*[26]

For Reflection:
As you read chapter six what did you:

    Hope?

    Remember?

26. *Chocolat*, DVD, directed by Lasse Hallström.

Think?

Pray?

As you consider developing a new monastic community that is anchored in your congregation, what would be the best form of community?

Where are the abandoned places of empire where you live?

What do you think would be the top three challenges to forming a new monastic community that is anchored in your church? How would you recommend engaging these challenges?

In the movie, *Chocolat*, a very religious town is transformed by practices of hospitality. What can the United Methodist Church learn about community transformation from this movie, and how does it relate to what you have learned about new monasticism?

Acts 2:37–47 and 5:12–16 describe a Christian community in which table fellowship is an essential element of spiritual community. What is the relationship of table fellowship, the liturgical practice of communion, and the formation of powerful Christian communities?

SIX

Reports from the Horizon

Scripture Reading: Philippians 2:1–13
Hymn: Whom Shall I Send? (582, *United Methodist Hymnal*)

Recommended Movie: *Gran Torino*[27]

For Reflection:
As you read chapter six what did you:
    Hope?

    Remember?

    Think?

    Pray?

Now that you have read *Longing for Spring*, what (if any) concrete actions do you feel called toward in your own life? In the life of your congregation?

When you watched the movie, *Gran Torino*, which parts of the story connected with the ethos of the new monasticism? What can United Methodists learn from *Gran Torino*?

27. *Gran Torino*, DVD, directed by Clint Eastwood.

Philippians 2:6–11 is one of the earliest hymns of the church, the "kenotic" hymn. "Kenosis" is a Greek word that means self-emptying. What are the ways in which new monasticism helps the rest of the church to learn to live a kenotic life?

In the space below, write a prayer that reflects what you feel, think, remember, and hope for your life and for the church in light of what you have learned in this study:

The Role of the Anchor Church

What exactly is the role of the anchor church? How should new monastic communities relate to the anchor church and vice versa? There are several ways a fruitful connection can take place. It is important for each anchor church and its new monastic community to discern the parameters of their connection. What is best in one situation may not work in another. A "cookie cutter" approach, which is a temptation in our denomination, is doomed to fail. We really do need to listen to what the Spirit is saying to the church in each situation.

A good relationship depends upon creating a connection that is for the mutual well-being of the church and the monastic community. The anchor church should not be exploitive, controlling, or disengaged. It should be nurturing and prayerful toward the community. The community should cultivate hospitality and friendship toward the anchor church.

Let's talk about money first. The new monastic community does not exist in order to raise money for the anchor church and its budget, nor does the anchor church exist as a pocket book for the new monastic community's outreach projects. If a team of bi-vocational pastors lead the new monastic community and they meet for worship in a house or some other borrowed space, and the ministries of the community are carried out by the members of the community, that eliminates most of the cost of ministry other than what is being spent in outreach. Because the bi-vocational leaders are giving up a salary for ministry, living kenotically, and the community members are doing likewise, it is appropriate to ask the anchor church and denominational officials to also practice kenosis in refraining from asking the new monastic communities to use their financial resources to fund the anchor church. Let the new monastic communities use their money to reach out in mission to their neighbors near and far. Let them use all of their giving for mission. This will present a powerful, kenotic face of the church to a watching world.

If money is not the tie that binds, then what should connect the anchor church to the community? Prayer, spiritual formation, and mission. For example, the senior pastor or some other pastor on staff who has responsibility for mission and outreach could meet monthly with the pastoral team from the new monastic community for mutual spiritual formation. It could be an old-fashioned Wesleyan band meeting. The pastor of the anchor church and the pastoral team of the community would meet as colleagues and siblings in Christ, sharing prayer, encouragement, and emotional support. They could engage in common readings or follow the same rule of life together.

Another fine connection is for the anchor church to host the new monastic community twice a year during a worship gathering in which the community leads the worship and provides the message to the anchor church. A celebratory meal could follow. During the announcement time of the worship gathering, the community could let the anchor church know about upcoming mission activities in which the anchor church could participate, such as a work day on a Habitat house or a retreat day for at risk students who are the missional focus of the new monastic community.

Similarly, the monastic community would welcome anchor church members as guests from time to time in the community's worship or at its evening prayer once a week, or for a retreat day at the monastic house. Thus, the monastic community could help the anchor church members grow deeper in their spiritual practices and in learning how to use a daily office and practice hospitality in their own neighborhoods.

A bulletin board and bulletin inserts could keep the anchor church abreast of news and ministry that is going on in the monastic community, so as to be able to pray for and encourage community members. The anchor church should think of the new monastic community as a missionary community that just happens to live close to the anchor church instead of in a country far away.

Members of the new monastic community could come to the church several times a year to lead a Bible study, teach a segment of a membership class, guest teach a Sunday School class, or offer some other event to help the anchor church cultivate a missional ecclesiology in its neighborhood. That is, the community members would help to open the imagination of the anchor church.

If an anchor church develops a network of several new monastic communities, once or twice a year all the communities could join together with the anchor church for a worship celebration and meal, and stories of God's work that is taking place in all of their ministries.

These are just a few recommendations, but not exhaustive by any means. With some creativity and prayer, I am confident that a healthy, mutually enriching relationship can be formed for the glory of God.

BIBLIOGRAPHY

Adams, M. Clare. "Religious Life." In *The New Dictionary of Catholic Spirituality*. Edited by Michael Downey, 817–22. Collegeville, MN: Liturgical, 1993.

Arias, Mortimer. *Announcing the Reign of God: Evangelization and the Subversive Memory of Jesus*, 1984. Reprint, Lima, OH: Academic Renewal, 2001.

Athanasius. *The Life of St. Anthony*. Translated by Robert Gregg. New York: Paulist, 1980.

Benedict of Nursia. *Rule of St. Benedict*. Translated with introduction and notes by Anthony C. Meisel and M. L. Mastro. Garden City: Image, 1975.

Bessenecker, Scott A. *The New Friars: The Emerging Movement Serving the World's Poor*. Downer's Grove, IL: InterVarsity, 2006.

Bonhoeffer, Dietrich. *Life Together*. Translated with an introduction by John W. Doberstein. San Francisco: HarperSanFrancisco, 1954.

———. *Testament to Freedom*. San Francisco: HarperSanFrancisco, 1997.

Bosch, David J. *Transforming Mission: Paradigm Shifts in Theology of Mission*. American Society of Missiology Series 16. Maryknoll, NY: Orbis, 1991.

Bowie, Fiona, editor. *Beguine Spirituality: Mystical Writing of Mechthild of Magdeburg, Beatrice of Nazareth, and Jadewijch of Brabant*. Translated by Oliver Davies. New York: Crossroad, 1990.

Brown, Dale W. *Understanding Pietism*. Grand Rapids: Eerdmans, 1978.

Bucer, Martin. *Instruction in Christian Love*. Translated by Paul Traugott Fuhrman. Richmond: Knox, 1952.

Burnett, Amy Nelson. *The Yoke of Christ: Martin Bucer and Christian Discipleship*. Ann Arbor: Edwards, 1994.

Campbell, Ted A. *Methodist Doctrine: The Essentials*. Nashville: Abingdon, 1999.

———. *Religion of the Heart: A Study of Religious Life in the Seventeenth and Eighteenth Century*. Columbia: University of South Carolina Press, 1991.

Chittister, Joan. *Wisdom Distilled from the Daily: Living the Rule of St. Benedict Today*. San Francisco: Harper & Row, 1990.

Chocolat. Directed by Lasse Hallström. Miramax Films, 2001. DVD.

Christian Community Development Association. "Christian Community Development Association." No pages. Online: http://www.ccda.org/.

Claiborne, Shane. *Irresistible Revolution: Living as an Ordinary Radical*. Grand Rapids: Zondervan, 2006.

Claiborne, Shane, and Jonathan Wilson-Hartgrove. *Becoming the Answer to Our Prayers: Prayer for Ordinary Radicals.* Downer's Grove, IL: InterVarsity, 2008.

Cole, Neil. *Organic Church: Growing Faith Where Life Happens.* San Francisco: Jossey-Bass, 2005.

Day, Dorothy. *The Long Loneliness: The Autobiography of Dorothy Day.* Chicago: Saint Thomas More, 1993.

Dickson, Doug. "Facebook: The New Methodists." Online: http://www.facebook.com/home.php#/group.php?gid=9550978460.

Estep, William. *The Anabaptist Story: An Introduction to Sixteenth Century Anabaptism.* Grand Rapids: Eerdmans, 1996.

Forest, Jim. "Introduction." In *Mother Maria Skobtsova: Essential Writings*, 23. Maryknoll, NY: Orbis, 2003.

Gerdes, Egon, "Theological Tenets of Pietism." *The Covenant Quarterly* (Feb/May 1976) 25.

Gibbs, Eddie, and Ryan K. Bolger. *Emerging Churches: Creating Christian Community in Postmodern Cultures.* Grand Rapids: Baker, 2005.

Goeters, Johann Friedrich Gerhard. "Der reformierte Pietismus in Deutschland 1650–1690." In *Der Pietismus von siebzehnten bis zum frühen achtzehnten Jahrhundert*, edited by Martin Brecht et al., 241–77. Geschichte des Pietismus 1. Göttingen: Vandenhoeck & Ruprecht, 1993.

Gran Torino. Directed by Clint Eastwood. Warner Home Video, 2009. DVD.

Gregory the Great. *Dialogues of Gregory the Great, Book 2: Saint Benedict.* Translated with an introduction and notes by Myra Uhlfelder. Indianapolis: Bobbs-Merrill, 1967.

Halter, Hugh, and Matt Smay. *The Tangible Kingdom: Creating Incarnational Community.* San Francisco: Jossey-Bass, 2008.

Hardt, Phillip. *The Soul of Methodism: The Class Meeting in Early New York Methodism.* Lanham, MD: University of America Press, 2000.

Harmless, William. *Desert Christians: An Introduction to the Literature of Early Monasticism.* Oxford: Oxford University Press, 2004.

Heath, Elaine. *The Mystic Way of Evangelism: A Contemplative Vision for Christian Outreach.* Grand Rapids: Baker, 2008.

———. *Naked Faith: The Mystical Theology of Phoebe Palmer.* Princeton Theological Monograph Series. Eugene, OR: Pickwick, 2009.

Hirsch, Alan. *The Forgotten Ways: Reactivating the Missional Church.* Grand Rapids: Brazos, 2006.

Jesus Camp. Directed by Heidi Ewing and Rachel Grady. Magnolia Films, 2007. DVD.

Jones, Tony. *The New Christians: Dispatches from the Emergent Frontier.* A Living Way. San Francisco: Jossey-Bass, 2008.

Koinonia Partners. "Koinonia." Online: http://www.koinoniapartners.org/whatis.html.

Lawrence, William B. *Methodism in Recovery: Renewing Mission, Reclaiming History, Restoring Health.* Nashville: Abingdon, 2008.

Kinnaman, David, and Gabe Lyons. *Unchristian: What a New Generation Thinks about Christianity . . . and Why It Matters.* Grand Rapids: Baker, 2007.

Kisker, Scott Thomas. *Foundation for Revival: Anthony Horneck, the Religious Societies, and the Construction of an Anglican Pietism.* Lanham, MD: Scarecrow, 2007.

Matheson, George. "O Love That Wilt Not Let Me Go." In *The United Methodist Hymnal*, 480. Nashville: United Methodist, 1989.

McDonnell, Ernest W. *Beguines and Beghards in Medieval Culture, with Special Emphasis on the Belgian Scene.* New York: Octagon, 1969.

McLaren, Brian. *A Generous Orthodoxy.* Grand Rapids: Zondervan, 2004.

The Mission. Directed by Roland Joffé. Warner Home Video, 1986. DVD.

Newbigin, Lesslie. *The Household of God: Lectures on the Nature of the Church.* London: SCM, 1953.

New Day. "The People of New Day." Online: http://newdaydallas.org/.

Oliver, Mary. "In Blackwater Woods." In *American Primitive,* 82. Boston: Back Bay, 1983.

The Order of Saint Benedict. "The Rule of Benedict." Online: http://www.osb.org/rb/.

Oyer, John S. "Bucer Opposes the Anabaptists." Mennonite Quarterly Review 68 (1994) 24–50.

Patch Adams. Directed by Tom Shadyac. Universal Studios, 2003. DVD.

Podmore, Colin. *The Moravian Church in England, 1728–1760.* Oxford: Clarendon, 1998.

Richey, Russell E. *Early American Methodism.* Religion in North America. Bloomington: University of Indiana Press, 1991.

Rutba House. *School(s) for Conversion: 12 Marks of a New Monasticism.* Eugene, OR: Cascade, 2005.

School for Conversion. "New Monasticism." Online: http://www.newmonasticism.org.

The Secret Life of Bees. Directed by Gina Prince-Bythewood. 20th Century Fox, 2009. DVD.

St. Cuthbert's House. "Northumbria Community." Online: http://www.northumbria community.org/.

Sine, Tom. *The New Conspirators: Creating the Future One Mustard Seed at a Time.* Downers Grove, IL: InterVarsity, 2008.

Stock, Jon, et al. *Inhabiting the Church: Biblical Wisdom for a New Monasticism.* New Monastic Library. Eugene, OR: Cascade, 2007.

Thompson, Marjorie J. *Soul Feast.* Louisville: Westminster John Knox, 2005.

Tickle, Phyllis. *The Great Emergence: How Christianity Is Changing and Why.* Grand Rapids: Baker, 2008.

Tucker, Ruth A., and Walter L. Liefeld. *Daughters of the Church: Women and Ministry from New Testament Times to the Present.* Grand Rapids: Zondervan, 1987.

The United Methodist Church. *The Book of Discipline of the United Methodist Church 2004* [CD ROM]. Nashville: Abingdon, 2004.

The United Methodist Church. *The Book of Discipline of the United Methodist Church.* Nashville: United Methodist, 2008.

The United Methodist Hymnal. Nashville: United Methodist, 1989.

United Methodist Young Clergy. "United Methodist Young Clergy." Online: http://www .umcyoungclergy.com.

Van Engen, John, editor. *Devotio Moderna: Basic Writings.* Classics of Western Spirituality. New York: Paulist, 1983.

Van Zijl, Theodore P. *Gerard Groote: Ascetic ad Reformer.* Washington, DC: Catholic University of America Press, 1963.

Veilleaux, Armand, translator. *The Life of Saint Pachomius and His Disciples.* Cistercian Studies Series 45. Kalamazoo, MI: Cistercian, 1980.

Ward, W. R. *The Protestant Evangelical Awakening.* Cambridge: Cambridge University Press, 1992.

Warner, Laceye C. *Saving Women: Retrieving Evangelistic Theology and Practice.* Waco: Baylor University Press, 2007.

Watson, David Lowes. *Early Methodist Class Meeting: Its Origins and Significance.* Nashville: Discipleship Resources, 1985.

Watson, Kevin M. *A Blueprint for Discipleship: Wesley's General Rules as a Model for Christian Living.* Nashville: Discipleship Resources, 2009.

Weems, Lovett H., Jr. "Are Young Elders Disappearing?" *Circuit Rider* (March/April 2006) 6–7.

Weinlick, John R. *Count Zinzendorf.* Nashville: Abingdon, 1966.

Wesley, John. Journal entry from March 13, 1743. In *The Works of John Wesley,* vol. 19. Edited by Reginald Ward and Richard Heitzenrater. Nashville: Abingdon, 1989.

———. "The Nature Design and General Rules of the United Societies." In *The Works of John Wesley,* vol. 9. Edited by Rupert Davies. Nashville: Abingdon, 1989.

———. "Of the Church." In *The Works of John Wesley,* vol. 3. Edited by Albert Outler. Nashville: Abingdon, 1986.

———. "Plain Account of the People Called Methodists." In *The Works of John Wesley,* vol. 9. Edited by Rupert Davies. Nashville: Abingdon, 1989.

———. "Signs of the Times." In *The Works of John Wesley,* vol. 2. Edited by Albert Outler. Nashville: Abingdon, 1985.

Wilson-Hartgrove, Jonathan. *To Baghdad and Beyond: How I Got Born Again in Babylon.* Eugene, OR: Cascade, 2005.

———. *Free to Be Bound: Church Beyond the Color Line.* Colorado Springs: NavPress, 2008.

———. *New Monasticism: What it Has to Say to Today's Church.* Grand Rapids: Brazos, 2008.

Wink, Walter. *The Powers that Be: Theology for the New Millennium.* New York: Doubleday, 1998.